WILD LADY

Freedom From Strategic Sadistic Abuse

First Part

Ewa Lawresh

10-10-10
Publishing

Dedication

From a mom who is a Wild Lady now for my two kids

For my two daughters, that they know...

what sadistic strategic (collective) abuse on one girl/woman is – a mother of two, who, as a sadist's scapegoat, had to publicly 'burn' on all the eyes of excited sadistic beholders, pay for (collective) sadists': projections (psychological/ body-based), toxic shame, illusions, madness, insecurities, jealousy – in total as their collective subconscious. This, which happened publicly to her, is a case to the Supreme Court.

It's a book about HER – a healthy innocent (who was lost because of childhood and life traumas and at the end will meet her inner hello, and maybe, one day... outer hello...) who was dragged into sadistic persecutory societies which form a sadistic psychiatric hospital based on persecution, punitive settlements and submission (though never human attitude based on compassion and divine love). Sadistic persecutory societies operate from toxic shame, illusions, madness, insecurities, and jealousy, which reside in sadists' inner smallness, constantly pumped into their inner poisoned incarcerated hatred that wants to eat them like cancer from inside. So from this place of who they are – they act... they act with this inner cancer from the power over upon an innocent...

For my two daughters that they know WHY...

the real wild woman has been destroyed on this planet for centuries, and why she still exists in me

your mom, Ewa

***

I dedicate this book also to every innocent, kind-hearted, genuine human on this planet who was ever a targeted object of a sadist; those who, as innocent people, experienced relational sadistic abuse, which was strategically planned behind their back. The book is for the ones who were unaware that such sadism was even possible...

Chapters with nr "0" represent the beginning and the end – born, death, reborn, death, as we are alive on point zero – where is the balance, with no beginning and no end – only particles in life (for example, 0 process – 0 process – 0 process – 0 process, etc. – zero does not mean 'small' or 'low'). It's all about human evolution – measured in participant for the same exact participant. It's never between another participant and another participant.

Table of Contents

Introduction

May I invite you to consider...

The biggest issue in all strategic sadistic abuse is the release of the sadism itself on an innocent and vulnerable person who is not a masochist. Why? Children are not masochists, although those who experienced sadism when their system was still being formed, from those who were raising them, experienced co-dependent attachment to this same intensity. When this intensity is reactivated in the child's system, it opens compulsion, which is an addiction to experiencing the same intensity experienced before, even if the child does not like it and feels unhappy. All is not by choice. Instead, all is by programming and unconscious conditions. I invite you to consider, when you read this book, coming to connection with yourself if you have ever before felt what you feel when you are reading this book and contemplate what happened in your own life in terms of sadism and stress based on childhood adverse experiences being at the same time surrounded by sadists. Please consider whether this was put on you behind your back without your awareness, or you were aware of what was happening, as evidenced by the begging for it to stop. Maybe you are the sadist carrying the traits of feeling enormous power over the victim who suffers. You look for any way to laugh at when the victim is humiliated, degraded and fully dehumanized. Maybe that gives you a relief somehow that it's not happening to you, that this has escaped you, that you have the power to feel contempt and pride over the other. You feel quite well, quite calm for a moment, until you have to repeat this sadistic cycle again and again towards the innocent one. If you are a sadist, you can find your strategies here and, if possible, reflect... I wish you could reflect on what you have done, and I feel it's not only me as your victim speaking here through my voice. In this book, the words 'the child', 'the innocent one', 'the victim', and 'the scapegoat' have the same meaning – as the vulnerable one and out of defence. Through this book, I want to help people all over the world, wherever they live, whatever gender, sexuality, or nationality; whatever beliefs they have about themselves, so that they go inside either being the sadists or the innocent one turned by the sadists towards a complete private misery or complete public smash through prosecution and persecution. Creating a life without sadism is a very hard journey...

with all my love.

So... you say, you know me... more, you say you know who I am... I will tell you something:
...A girl is never a whore. A girl is a child.
...A raped girl is never a slut. A raped girl is a paedophile's/kidnapper's victim.

...A raped woman is not a prostitute. A raped woman is a rapist's victim.

Some words ("slut," "whore," "prostitute," etc.) used in the social arena after following sadists' mind representation can be explained below for educational purposes: slut, whore, prostitute (you name it) who is raped – is a raped human.

For the sadists it's always fun, for the innocent one it's always cruelty.

Foreword

What do you think is the reason you were born? Have you ever wondered if the life you lead is truly yours? Have you ever trusted any institution, organisation, or other group of people who had certified titles, and believed that they had the right to make decisions about your life as a group with authority? Perhaps you lead your life unconsciously, based on past programming, without realising that it's not your life, but a life that was created unconsciously –from the place where others wanted you to live.

Finding out who you genuinely are takes time, but it's worth it. When you love yourself, you can lead the life you want. In *Wild Lady,* Ewa Lawresh shares her years of experience to increase awareness about women's rights, and what it means NOT to have women's rights. No matter what trauma you may have experienced, there is a way out. You were not born a scapegoat. Your authentic true self is awaiting you.

Ewa Lawresh has come through a long journey full of trauma and devastating adverse childhood experiences. She has worked for more than 18 years in the area of human evolution and, like a phoenix, is rising again. This is a courageous woman whose attitude to stay true to herself helped her win all the battles she faced. In this book, you will find guidelines and suggestions that you can follow to help you find yourself, and transform your life for yourself.

Raymond Aaron
New York Times Bestselling Author

Chapter 0

'Prenatal Mind' WOMB / Sadism

I f there were a created project called "About 'Me', Without Me", this project would perfectly fit the public show that happened in the reputation arena about 'me' without me. Show without a person in it is about not this innocent person but about the collective subconscious into which this innocent person is dragged by the sadists (without 'me' in it, without 'my' awareness/consciousness, without being informed – there has to be an expression for this...).

What is that exactly about? It is being a centre of attention to become a public trash bin for the reason to be falsely accused. It's happening through false allegations and psychological projections without any factual proof. It is all done by being put on trials and under psychological tortures from anyone who wishes to participate in it, including individuals and groups (cults, communities, organisations, institutions, societies, and systems). My life was destroyed through criminal use, abuse and exploitation of my personal data, authorship inventions and intellectual property by many while it was spread without my consent. These all were used and abused for profit for others (rather than mine) and never ever protected. I was not credited for the work and the impact I have made based on my own ideas and brain resolutions.

I was recorded without consent, and this exposition was out of context. What happened to me was against human rights and data (intellectual property) protection rights and was done by sadists, grandiose and malicious narcissists, psychopaths and sociopaths, murderers and criminals.

I call them all sadists, as they all have unmanaged, repressed sexual energy. What happened to me publicly was a result of sadists' repressed energy based on their bodily, not processed, energy level. If a person is in energetic balance on a body level, such person does not destroy an innocent person's life, and also does not enjoy other person's pain. In this context, all of my perpetrators land in one category – sadism.

Sadists have no capacity to FEEL and exist in reality. Inside of them, there is no capacity to love or feel loving kindness, but they have a huge capacity to control (from the death place inside of them), which is fake power over everything and everyone. They never act from a place of humanity and compassion, as they cannot embrace being an alive (childlike) human living on this planet.

You have to understand that sadists have an obsession with faces – they have to look better than you in terms of public reputation, or they have to destroy your reputation. Sadists launch on your life when you are in misery by inflicting psychological tortures because they are JEALOUS and in HATRED. It's called living life under a previously mentioned project about "you" without truly you in it.

Ewa: SADISTS, WHAT ARE YOU DOING WITH MY LIFE?
Sadists: We are building our lives at your cost, and we are taking advantage of you when you are not aware of what we are doing... so this way we are rising in sadistic abuse – we call it justice.
Ewa: Really? What if you all made a mistake about me? What if everything you have seen about me was actually about you?

Sadists live in the past, and only in the past. They never see what is NOW as they do not exist in NOW. Sadists like destroying the literal red face of an innocent person (*I Will Tell, Anyway!* by Ewa Lawresh) or public face no matter which way it is done. My life was destroyed because I have a different way of thinking about being a woman born with a diverse mind – only because of it...

What is the cost of destroying somebody's car? What is the cost of destroying somebody's brain? What is the cost of destroying somebody's life because of a destroyed brain?

Everything is about the process into reality in NOW. It's not about bodily level after all, while collectively, this is what happened to me was and still is manifesting in sadists on the bodily level. So it's not about the body itself but rather the mind and its rigidity. To help self is important, turning through softness into wildness. What is needed is a healthy mind as wildness, pure innocence and a divine place inside of human – in this place ambiguity is not bringing confusion or sites. Here is harmony and a balanced healthy wild mind based on resilient thinking.

A wild mind brings mental health; a rigid mind brings mental illness.

Sadism is something inside the perpetrator and is based on survival, manifesting through looking for power over the targeted innocent person. The perpetrator feels contempt towards the victim and wishes to persecute and punish the innocent target and take from the innocent target everything possible to build their own life – based on the persecution of innocence. Through contempt, sadists intimidate, humiliate, degrade, harass, belittle the innocent one, who first has to be slowly and unpredictably weakened by the sadists from their own power and protection. After this, sadists degrade innocent ones to the level of misery/distress/vexation/pang/torment and tortures of any kind. The innocent target is pushed many times through this adversity and is unaware of being manipulated. Anything that the innocent says will be turned against them, but they do not know it.

Inner sadism is based on inner adversity, manifesting inside of the sadist who has power over others in relationships, family, institutional or social systems. This adversity happens inside the sadists through their obsessive desire for sadistic release intertwined with sadistic excitement and empowerment felt over the innocent. Sadism is not healthy for the sadists (and, of course, for the victim). That is why they act sadism out to receive inner release based on survival, animal body, out of any logic. The main purpose for the sadists is to feel at the end sexual release – symbolic or non-symbolic. Sadistic desire does not have to be conscious, but all are driven by their disconnection on their body level. Symbolic resale is like the entrance to repressed sexual energy inside. Sadists feel lower than their victims because they do not take responsibility for who they are. They feel envy, jealousy, and their own smallness, so they release their sadistic energy on the innocent.

Have you ever met a sadist? Have you ever experienced strategic sadistic abuse? Have you ever felt humiliated to the point of having a red face, feeling so dehumanised and so ashamed, and at the same time observing and feeling their sadistic laughter on your own skin? Have you ever felt intense pain in your ears due to their sadistic roaring?

No matter what happened to you through strategic sadistic abuse, it is possible to heal and reach a place where you come from survival existence to a place of safety within you. In my opinion, based on my own lifetime experience, there are two ways of coming out from strategic sadistic abuse. The first way is that you will get out from survival into safety that, in the end, this survival mode will vanish from your nervous system (hopefully you will get out from this fully healthy, and if not, then with some "gifts" like chronic illness or brain damage, etc.). The second way is that you will simply die. There are no other ways experienced by me till now. I want to be honest with you in this book, as honesty and truthfulness are the only possible ways for me to live on this planet.

The horrific, hideous human journey I experienced was served to me by the sadists from the so-called Western society. Throughout my entire life, I have never felt seen or understood. I was born in Western society within Western lifestyle – with its specific norms, ethics, values, beliefs and ways of behaviour. And yet I have never ever felt seen or understood by the Western society. I was not born in an Eastern society with an Eastern lifestyle and specifics. However, seeing the world from the diverted mind as a cisgender woman, I feel closer to Eastern culture in many ways because of my accepting attitude towards diversity. I have a different way of seeing the world from early childhood and embracing humanity, compassion, and kindness as the highest values (which do not come to me from Western society). All I see is not based on beliefs but rather on my observation and unique lifetime experience. Western culture and Eastern culture differ enormously from each other, though they are in a slow intertwining process. I feel that I do not belong now to either of these two worlds as a duality, but rather what is forming for me in me is one new better world from a place of wholeness. A diverted mind allowed me to see differently and separate myself safely by making different choices. In this book, wild means 'resilient mind,' which allows one to be alive in body and live from freed spirit – the mind that sees differently from most minds. This way belongs to diversity rather than the singularity of the collective subconscious.

Between feminine surrender and masculine penetration, there is balanced sovereignty – this way wild, healthy Lady is born.

In this book, I am not talking about consensual sadism in sexual relationships, which some people prefer and choose as consenting adults.

I am talking in this book about sadism which is non-consensual and can last for many years, or even for all of the victim's life, while the victim is unaware that it is being strategically done. It is a trap for the victim, a trap often without a way out. In this book, you can learn how to extricate yourself from sadistic abuse. It's all about growing up and maturing so that you can rebuild after childhood adversity and re-parent yourself into an adult who is relationally free from the other as an individual with their own uniqueness, integrated wholeness as one, self-leadership and self-energy management (without depending on any other person, their beliefs or their mind's structure) or even entire system as a failed human construct. Sadism is about inflicting cruelty as a punitive and persecutory sadistic way to gain power over the innocent. So the question appears, how can you heal after experiencing this type of cruelty, and how can you successfully reach the place of inner safety and peace inside of you? How can you find your dignity and understand and love yourself?

I will try to show you from the depths of my heart how I see sadistic strategic abuse from my own life experience and what could be helpful for you to understand yourself in the dynamics of such an abusive dance with the sadists planted already in your own life.

You have to remember that sadists want you to experience *their* own life and *their* own misery. No happy and fulfilled person is a sadist and acts towards innocence in a sadistic way. Sadists want you to live *their* miserable life and be like *them*. Sadists want you to suffer but mostly to commit suicide by yourself that there are no suspicions that it's the sadist's work. In most cases, the sadist is left with white gloves after all.

Sadism is always meant to directly or indirectly destroy the innocent person's public face and public/personal life. There are many strategies that sadists use to destroy an innocent person. Strategic sadistic abuse is based on imputing a high level of stress in prolongation in slow motion with some deviations as "bombs" from time to time that you frankly live from the place of unpredictability and the unknown. Innocent people can attract sadists if, in their childhood or teenage years, they had some basis in sadistic upbringing.

That means that if before seven years of age the person experienced sadism in childhood - from kids (this can be their older sibling or same age group of kids against one) or from adults like people in authority such as a parent till a government representative, such person as an innocent child is conditioned and addicted to looking subconsciously for people who will have sadistic traits inside because of inner intensity. They can attract this kind of people by not even inviting them into their own life. Childhood programming will be subconsciously reactivated only if this matches the same category of authority level pushed into the scapegoat as a way of power over actions exactly the same as those experienced in the earlier years of the scapegoat's life. All childhood programming can be reactivated even without an awareness of the innocent one, anyway.

Sadists charge on the victim's inner stress. Could you possibly imagine? Stress response in the innocent victim has its roots in the early place of existence – starting in a fetus. A stressed mother is a stressed environment for the child who is now in the mom's belly. A stressed child as the innocent is in the process of forming inside of her belly what is the layout from the beginning for the child, that through all their life they will choose subconsciously stressful environments in order to experience the same level of stress as a norm. An innocent person as an adult will attract this type of people who will repeat the same environment and experience for the innocent one. So let's look closer at this sadistic cycle. A sadistic person is constantly going inside of the victim into their stress level. Then the sadist is pumping the innocent person's energy in a relational level so high until the sadists themselves can reach the sadistic peak. From this place starts the sadists' sadistic release, and their sadistic backlash is poured on an innocent child or an innocent adult. I became a target of sadists in my life so many times that they can simply sadistically, from jealousy and hatred, place release on me. I became a trash bin for them, that they could pour this sadism on me while I was already pumped in stress-related co-dependency and threat that they would kill me – as sadists go to the end. Sadistic strategic abuse is based on hate, envy, jealousy and shame from sadists' unbelievable smallness pumped through toxic sexual energy in them, which is repressed and denied entirely to the place that they are so disconnected that they strategically plan sadism from the manipulatory aggressive mind. They plan this to the extent of removing the innocent from this planet. The sadist is inputting sadistic abuse while having themselves no capacity inside to love, and having no capacity to express love outside. All are based on their inner emptiness and feelings of shallow nervousness and frustration based on perverse obsession. From this place, they threaten the innocent as their target – an object of release. These types of dynamics give the sadist the omnipotent right to treat the innocent from a place of contempt sadistically. Sadists feel self-loathing and inner hatred – so from this place is rising sadistic mockery.

Sadists also charge on the victim's feeling of not being wanted. They do this through rejection in any possible form. When the innocent child is not wanted in a family of origin by primal caregivers and is directly informed about this, hearing this in any possible place in their life, such child will always feel unwanted and unwelcomed. And the innocent child will lose the sense of belonging and moreover will lose all the inner roots as a lost foundation from which to grow up and mature in any way. Not being welcomed can be expressed directly in such families towards the child's ears, for example, "The only reason you were not aborted was because of my religious fears." In this case, the child's existence is, in fact, based on the beliefs and scarcity of the mother in the face of these beliefs that she cannot "abort" the kid. The innocent child feels that their life exists only because someone held certain beliefs, and the main motive was that the outside face of the caregiver had to remain in positive "light." An unwanted child as an adult rises on conditioning towards being unwanted, unwelcomed and not loved. Such an innocent person can become surely a targeted object of the sadists, and such an innocent will likely be.

I was never chosen from love, but by sadistic users for sadistic usage and then when they were fully set up in their own lives and careers, I was always thrown away. Credit for the work I did the last 20 years of my life was taken on the sadists' behalf, who, to silence me, were trying to destroy my reputation and remove me from the market. Even being recorded without my awareness for somebody's purposes was a use for the sadists' aims and my public destruction. I have seen a few times that I have been recorded in a public place by somebody's cell phone. In this place was rising stress inside me unconsciously, and I was each time in shock, and my half-mutism (which I suffered almost all my life) was already reactivated as I was in a place of freeze, anyway.

In this book, I will not refer to any psychological knowledge or research, other people's ideas, other books, definitions or points of view based on other people's experiences. Everything in this book is written from my own experience, based on my own life and my journey until now.

Chapter 1

STRATEGIES of Sadistic Abuse – part 1

W hat you will read below is more about the way the sadists live their lives. Strategic sadistic abuse is based on threatening the victim to the place where the victim feels intimidation. This way, the sadist is weakening the innocent from their own self-protection, entirely ripping out slowly any layers of this self-protection. It's a mechanism. Everything in sadistic strategic abuse is based on weakening the victim.

The sadist is about to entrap the innocent through belittling and slow motion degradation, which means that the innocent in this way is strategically cached in this entrapment (inner trap based on traumatisation, stress response and sadist-co-dependency relation based on full of obedience and threat with no way out). The sadist, through repeated prolongation, weakens their prey more and more. The strategy is to degrade and humiliate the victim. The sadist is gaining power over through hidden agenda – sexual arousal in these circumstances as toxic sexual empowerment over the innocent. Innocence is not important for the sadist – innocence is the target, an object, a product, a tool for something to gain by destroying the innocence in time, gradually, step by step.

A threat-based strategy is used by sadists to pump stress inside an innocent person. Threat based relation, in this case, is then already evoked. In my case, this kind of relation between me as an innocent one and the sadist started already in my early childhood. When I decided to look for help as an adult and started healing childhood and early attachment wounds, sadists revoked this relation between themselves and me, identically to what happened to me throughout my entire childhood. Sadists, through triggering me in my reactivity, were also pumping their own stress. They used me as their object of attention (a trash bin, the object to be beaten and kicked). They used me as a so-called re-activator of it (a blamed object) and a receiver of their sadism. While suffering all my life from complex post-traumatic stress disorder, my stress level was pumped to the same level I did experience in my childhood at the exact moment of the blowout of the sadists' attacks. Sadists who took part in this objectification of me finally could, by mutual pumping in themselves towards me, pour everything in them onto me. They were coming to the place of blowing out from their own stress level, and then they were releasing all their inner sadism towards absolutely an innocent girl/woman.

Collective Strategic Sadistic Abuse

The globe as per its inhabitants is so widely destroyed already through collective sadism – a formed sadistic social group. This social group is creating 'one' and within this sadistic oneness smaller groups are set up (communities, organisations, institutions, charities, etc), as well as the smallest forms such as sadistic human triads. Collective sadism starts with one sadist towards the innocent, a pair of sadists towards the innocent, and then bigger and bigger groups. Collective sadism is already involving all the globe no matter age, race, nationality, religion, beliefs, gender or sexuality. Sadists are everywhere and are more among the population than could be even imagined. This is spread so widely already that collective is taking sadism as something normal rather than the innocent one as the normal one – who is vulnerable and who is begging for help, human rights, and being treated like a human – is not receiving this at all. Why? Because it's not normal in the sadistic collective society to see themselves as a society abnormal, but instead, there is a chosen singular one – A PROBLEM. When an innocent person is begging to be heard, this innocent one is simply dehumanised, humiliated and deleted from the entire society. Will this ever shift places as a global change (so a problem is a whole society rather than an innocent individual) – could you tell me...?

The perception of reactivated innocence or a frozen, disconnected one on a spectrum of being a victim – for the observers and recipients (even if it's, let say, a sadistic family system) – the observers of this system form a collective, so the participants of this collective will blame the innocent for the effect of the sadism (either reactivation or frozen state of survival). Through psychological tortures, the observed object was not born to sell fixed ideas (as something like this does not exist in a human aspect as a human is organic and not plastic!). If this happens – all the profit belongs to the targeted innocence to repay what happened to their innocence. The observed object is treated in a sadistic way even for facial expression, which is not the way it should be for the sadist – as it's not, for example, the effect the sadists want per the impact of the sadist's input. Can you imagine? The sadist can plan what impact put on the victim that there will appear an effect (what comes from survival as a sadistic way of living) – let's say a fixing tool the sadist wants to reach in the victim. Sadists do not feel themselves as human, so as well they do not see the other as a human and naturally (as there is zero nature in the sadist) do not know that human was not born to be sized. The human was born to be understood, seen and loved... and only to be loved that can say hello to themselves and others who also have humanity in innocence.

The whole collective as one system can be involved in sadistic abuse to such an extent that half of the planet or more would like to kill the innocent one. Sides are formed, after all... Sometimes are not formed at all... there is only one side, and this side is formed by sadists who collectively try to spread sadism onto innocence – through one innocent person. We have here collective responsibility, and collective action should be taken to protect the one who is innocent. I have had this experience from my early childhood through all my life till now... I was always the observed target, the manipulated target, the target which is to be touched, to be researched, to be dragged out, to be commented based on sadistic illusions through mental constructs happening inside and only inside of the sadists, and they are exposed from their mouths as gossip and lies... the targeted object which is belittled and treated with contempt... can you imagine? Do you see yourself in this?

Sadism is an obsession based on attachment to the illusion - imaginary (based in mind) god of the cult. This poisoned attachment is in dimensions spread like a net inside the sadist. The more the sadist is attached to the figure of the cult, and their own grandiose is in this, the more the sadist will sadistically act from a sadistic mind - and from this place starts obsessed judgement and obsessed lies.

Sadists rise on the innocence (they NEVER protect innocence) - they rise their communities for the matter of bettering their own wealth, whatever that means for them - but mostly, it means strengthening falsely to hide their own shame. As a target of sadism, I was the one they were charging under repressed sexual energy, which has nothing to do with aliveness. Their charging is based on shame - even for the matter of criminal activity as, for example, till they record the innocent one to expose them through the toxic shame that the innocence is burning on the eye of the sadism. No one reacts - all laugh at the inner ridiculing state of the inner sadist. The usage of somebody's face/voice/ body/ideas - everything will be taken, and this is a crime - through copyrights and safety life violation of the innocent one. All will be used for money. Many sadists can call this -

for a higher matter. How is it that many probably believe that the Holocaust was also for the higher matter... probably from the perspective of those who were laughing – while trying to find a proper pose, preparing themselves to be pictured standing in the middle of the camp around piles of the dead bodies of the innocent...

The collective sadists are raised on the objectification of womanhood as a targeted piece of meat – from the place of power over. Sadistic perpetrators say and also have then this sadistic attitude which follows what they say: "It's only a woman... she only has a hole." In this place, my womanhood was denied for forming me a public "John." Sadists will even change your gender behind your back to gain sadistic satisfaction. Raping woman boundaries is an easy strategy for the sadists as when there is power over she is "done." And she is 'done' as it's a symbolic rape and also an invasion. Sadists want the victim's destruction even if this involves the victim's lifelong disability, stroke or damaged brain, chronic illness, burned face or whole body or even the innocent victim's death.

In the last years, what happened to me publicly, I call this collective sadistic strategic abuse. And when all of that was happening, I constantly was asking myself, WHERE AM I IN ALL OF THIS? THESE ARE NOT MY STORIES, AND IT'S DEFINITELY NOT ABOUT ME. I AM NOT THERE. But sadists did not see I was not in their sadistic stories. They were in their sadistic stories... They talk about somebody, and this somebody does not exist – well, only in their sadistic head. They talk about something that is inside of them. They talk about mental constructs based on their own sadistic rigid mind (rather *wild*) created on rigid beliefs from the closed box's narrow angles.

So what's happening in the last years ... it's happening through a revolution that many people have a place to scream their own trash onto the innocent object which is not any more for them a human – but a "whore", a "trash bin" etc. And they constantly try to put this trash on the other, while this trash is in themselves. And the more they are in sadism, the more creative sadistic lies they invent about the targeted object – the centre of their sadistic obsession.

Sadist's Scapegoat

So why is one person's life destroyed for the matter of the sadistic, abusive observer? First, sadists need a scapegoat. A scapegoat in a family system or sadistic social system is a person who will take the trash of the whole family/society because all is put on the scapegoat ("Whew, it's not me that this is happening – I will at least steal the apple from the show..." etc.).

In my case, to become a scapegoat was supported in this way that as a child, I took it that "...it's my fault... that it's because of me and always will be because of me" (*I Will Tell, Anyway!* by Ewa Lawresh). The child takes responsibility all their life for the disaster of the child's parents' marriage and all that has happened between the parents, and the child takes it as their fault.

For sadists, the show becomes normal – from now on, the targeted object is sharing "for free..." Why? Because sadists want for free so the innocent one is being recorded without consent... for example. What about data protection law/defamation protection law, etc.? Or do some have data protection and others not? Shared among all 'for free'... shared by the sadists that the sadists can go to "spa" or vacation spot... Remember: non-consensual sharing for profit of somebody's body, ideas, visual image, or voice – is a crime. You cannot "borrow" somebody's idea and make a profit on it and then, as per "borrowing," bring it back to the owner. Unless you pay royalties/profit directly to the inventor/author, it's a crime. From now on, the innocent person is shared for free (visually shared for free as some already are making business on the innocent human under traumatisation out of any consent) – so now she can spread her legs, and all can watch. More, everything will be at her personal cost, if she has kids, and her kids' cost. From now on, sadists can raise on her innocence and her non-consensual sharing "for free" invented by the sadists! When you read this... what is this reminding you about?

Isn't this happening under kidnapping and sex exploitation/trafficking – sharing for free a girl? They catch the victim and exploit – for free, at the victim's cost (her life energy, health, her life itself...). It's always at the victim's cost – for the matter of the one main person or the whole group who is profiting from the victim, anyway. For sure, there is never a consent. For god's sake, NEVER!

How is the scapegoat created? How is the problem in a

family system created? Which way is one child developing an illness, dysfunction or addiction in an unhealthy family system (in any system)? All the family system creates it as a place of tension for the child who takes it on themselves. The same thing is happening with sadistic communities, which pour on the scapegoat – what is important – is that this all is not true about the scapegoat, but it's all the truth about sadistic community/family system/social justice. A scapegoat is a vulnerable person who is so vulnerable that this vulnerable one has no protection to say "no." The scapegoat will also be sacrificed for the matter of communities to be destroyed so that the communities are not destroyed and "thrive" in their sadism. Can you imagine? It's patriarchal culture. It's a very important way of how the system supports the victim's abuse. When the child is conditioned this way and raised this way in a sadistic family system, this child will subconsciously repeat this program. While sadistic social justice will do their own work at the same time ("it's opportunity to make money on the victim as well as it's happening under kidnapping") – they will inflict sadism on the scapegoat, including amusement and laughter at, for the aftermath profit.

False Accusations of Harassment

1. He is so charming, he is so interested in me, he is so in love... he admires... he will give me a new life... he promises so much... I am opening myself and planning my

life with him... but he will hang me with this emotional turmoil... for him, it's rising on / profiting from the affection of the innocent person... I go to him as he said he is waiting for me... I go there... and he is closing his doors, accusing me falsely through his friend for attempt of harassment... He escapes and vanishes... I am left in sadism with his sadism... alone.

2. He wants me to work for him... he promises never to abuse me the way he was abused... he promises me heaven... I try my best, and I give my best. He is closing his doors in front of my face. No explanation, only threats from his friend... He escapes with my knowledge... and builds a career on it... he takes all the credit for my unique lifetime experience and knowledge also based on being tortured... And these doors in front of my nose – are closed now... I am left in sadism with his sadism... alone.

Harassment

As sadism is planned, false accusation of harassment is also planned as a tool by many. Sadism was strategically put on one woman who had many partners (as a consequence of being an incest victim in childhood in prolongation and repetition). Sadists, to destroy her life, used any possible data – true or false – to manipulate and use it for their own agenda (whatever that is) and used all this against her when she was under traumatisation. A sadistic group of people destroyed her life by spreading false information behind her back; for example, that she is a man who is abusing women while it was exactly the other way around! Which way does this happen? Let's see this closer – one woman is accusing the other woman of (non-existent) harassment from a place of hidden agenda – sadistic jealousy and sadistic envy. Strategic accusations of harassment are happening more and more as an abuse of law while even harassment is not taking place at all in these. Now how is it happening that people believe the one who is the accuser? So surprisingly, many people believed the sadists from a simple perspective – sadists had an authority position, the victim was in trauma, or sadists had many friends, the victim has a diverted mind and gets social life totally different than others, or maybe is on the autism spectrum/is introverted/was lastly abused by the friend who is now on the site of the sadists, etc.

False accusations of harassment – it's a strategy not only to dehumanise the victim but also to pump sadistic group arousal, which involves sadistic humiliation until the victim has a red face from inflicted tortures (so from false accusations/threat/humiliation) and all the sadists have sadistic release. Such situations appear till the death of the innocent one or till the 'red face' is on the innocent one – then sadists feel triumph as there is a visible effect – reactivation, red face, burned face, burned body, mutilation, hysteria... you name it. Sadists feel amusement from the signs that are different from normal/average in society; this means sadists can make from the victim, let's say, a puppet or a treasured animal in the circus. From drastic sadistic acts is abuse in a workplace where the boss will push the innocent one "to pay for all the humanity" because the innocent did not want to "be so loyal" as cynically "you are so loyal to me" to the edges of existence through sadistic extremes that the innocent will feel childhood red face again hanging upside down (*I Will Tell, Anyway!* by Ewa Lawresh). Shaming and humiliation are the biggest triumphs for the sadists. Sadists love hideous ordeals. They amuse them the most.

In my childhood, people in the women's body made me their own "pet"/'puppet.' And later on, in many places, this repeated again for me, from academia through all social life to work areas. Sadists are driven by sadistic power over and inner sadistic instincts. These sadistic instincts are based on thoughts formed inside the sadist's mind. Sadists cannot separate simple thoughts. They act upon these thoughts. If sadists or even the whole group as a collective from one working area feel hatred, contempt and jealousy towards the innocents, they will act from the place of their inner triggers, which will appear as accusations – and everything will be poured on the "pet"/'puppet.'

No, there was no consent in Australia for domination-submission dynamics with white supremacy towards one innocent person. No, I have never signed agreements (and there is no such consent given by me) to be anyone's pet. Accusations of harassment are very common. Unfortunately, they are so common to such an extent that of harassment are accused vulnerable men or vulnerable women who are being in this vulnerability in a state of love. My lifetime experience, if I had to count, would be that more people in women's bodies were sadistic towards me rather than people in men's bodies, while the trait can be among many expressed very differently.

Threat

I heard from my father, "If you tell anyone, I'll kill you" – that's the next strategy of the sadists. It's a threat, and as long as the child or victim of the sadist at any age is trapped from the inner place of the programmed sadistic upbringing – the victim has no place to go from the sadists into safety because it is so much conditioned and threat-based till feelings of terror and close to death inner state. The innocent one has to stay with the sadist from the survival perspective.

Sadists try to empower themselves with and from the authority place to show that they are somehow bigger than the victim and this creates dependency in the victim. Unfortunately, the child brought up by the sadists will unconsciously come into relational connection with sadists no matter what. Moreover, the victim will not even realise that this is a pattern and is already there, intertwined fully in the sadistic dance with the sadists.

Sadistic strategic abuse is inflicted on the innocent through time, in slow motion, in repetition, and in prolongation at the cost of the innocent one. Everything is at the cost of the innocent one. The sadist has to make sure first that the innocent one is vulnerable and is in a vulnerable place. This all creates entrapment as the innocent one feels all the suffering, which is the initial goal of the sadist. In this place, a sadist spreads the message like, "You will pay for all the humanity." Can you imagine? This message I received in 2018 and what the sadist said – the sadist did.

People who have an active cPTSD or PTSD can experience sadists in a horrific way as it's based on touching their stress level, which is from the sadistic perspective, the one key they use to activate the reactivation state in the victim what is so needed for the sadistic show. CPTSD, as a complex post-traumatic stress disorder, connects the victim's childhood, which literally is catapulting the victim into the childish place of existence and also losing reality between the exact age and the age of the entrapped sadism in their childhood. This creates the most extensive complexity for the victim, which can trap the innocent in the sadist's hook forever. An innocent person never deserves any form of abuse, moreover sadistic strategic abuse. The abuse I experienced was strictly more from the social one and, in some places, more from sociopaths rather than narcissists. Can a sadist with Hitler's traits project these traits onto the victim and treat the victim this way?

Chapter 2

STRATEGIES of Sadistic Abuse – part 2

2

Backstabbing

The next planned, fixated, rigid way of living from the sadistic perspective is that the innocent one deserves punishment. Have you ever wondered how the innocent scapegoat in the family system is created by the perpetrators? Which way is the scapegoat formed from the collective perspective within society? It's conditioned. First, the innocent child is made a scapegoat of sadism in the family system, while the perpetrator chooses the one who will take it on themselves. The sadist forces the one, consciously or unconsciously, through inter-winded situations inflicted by pain onto a child so that the child will lose themselves for the perpetrator – then the perpetrator has the chosen one by the backstab. The innocent one can lose who they truly are as the authentic one, so the real one is losing completely the inner identity of who they are as a child. The sadist formed the victim.

The sadistic perpetrator uses the child's dependency for their own purposes, soaking from the child like a slowly extruded sponge. The child is not seen by the sadists as a human from the beginning, so this way, the child also learns to treat themselves as not being a human, as the human rights were also denied to the child. The child becomes an innocent object on which the whole collective, later on, can charge – family/school/workplace sadistic systems including any possible sadistic communities (they NEVER protect innocence) – they all rise on the cost of the innocent one – they all rise on the innocence's vitality and simply on the innocence's aliveness energy. The sadists make the child a puppet, never by consent, always by force from the place of manipulation, gaslighting and most important, from the place of intimidation in the victim. So it's never a child's choice. It's a conditioned relational field where the child is only for one – for being exploited, abused and used to the last left piece like the piece of potato used on the potato grate in slow motion to the end... Sadistic strategic abuse is based on toxic shaming (which again is a form of punishment) on the innocent because the sadists are full of toxic shame inside, which is like a toxic poison in them. It can start very early for the innocent person to be called a "whore" in a family. The child does not even know at the beginning what this word means, and is born to be a "whore" or "slut" or any "product," even a sexual one. But the sadists will prove the innocent one that was born to be a "whore" by raping the innocent one in most cases from behind. This is created backstabbing. Backstabbing is one of the main characteristics of the sadist, which shows how small the sadists are – zero morals, zero ethics, all planned and all from behind. Sadists are full of toxic shame inside; they shame themselves for being backstabbers rather than front-equal partners and front-liners ready for equal negotiations. Backstabbers, as sadists, are proud of being this way. They even find being smarter than their innocent victim – as for the sadists backstabbing is proudness and pride to beat an unarmed, innocent person. Then backstabbers meet together to celebrate the triumph behind the scenes. The innocent one can be already dead, in hospital after tortures, or in the best circumstances is crying, lying on the floor being entirely left alone in this. When we observe this happening in sadistic groups, sadistic communities, sadistic family systems, and sadistic countries, there is the main mode in which the observer (the sadists) is more important than the actor (the innocent one), because the observer is mostly given power by somebody else and has an ORIENTATION ABOUT WHAT IS GOING ON. The observer is in a sadistic, narcissistic place in themselves to give this authority to use power over the vulnerable person who in most cases HAS ZERO IDEA ABOUT WHAT IS GOING ON AS THERE IS NO ORIENTATION. Sadism is based on backstabbing. And the question is, who is the guilty one – the vulnerable person or the system which supports this all?

Sadists will feel smarter than the innocent one only because the sadists think if they can cheat the innocent one as a way of backstabbing, it's a smart way of living (and this way of thinking is smart, and the innocent one is an "idiot" – again can you imagine?). An innocent one would never do this, even from a moral perspective. For the sadist, the innocent one is stupid as the innocent is not committing crimes like the sadist, who is "so smart to commit crimes on innocence." It's a massive paradox here, and blindness in this place of the sadist. How stupid the sadist is on the level of morals and ethics to position the innocent in life as a stupid one for the sake – how many crimes the sadist can commit around the innocent one. For this matter, a sadist will publicly show the innocent one that the innocent is an idiot. It's an inner idiot inside of the sadist who is doing this – as how stupid the person has to be, to be proud of being a criminal towards INNOCENCE!

Lost Innocent for the Abuser

The child loves the abuser and will justify the abuser until the place of dependency, mainly if the abuser will show at least sometimes some affection or care, which the child craves so much. So the child will choose to be with the abuser while losing all the care and love for themselves.

Sadistic strategic abuse is never about the child, and is never about the innocent person anyway. All is about the sadist while on the front line is always the innocent one – it's the one who is seen, so the one who is prosecuted and put here, whatever crime on the innocent one you wish to add... The sadist is the one who is hiding, at least the one who is behind all of this. This can be even the whole sadistic community, and what the sadist likes is to stay backstage collecting all possible profit on the innocent one. The example here is kidnapping, when the perpetrator takes money for the usage of the victim, while it can happen that the main perpetrator will not be seen and will not be involved in the process themselves (not to dirty their hands) – the sadistic perpetrator will involve others in this, even in any other case that the main sadist will only observe – will watch from a safe place for themselves. However, sadists will never care about the safety of the innocent one. This innocent child will subconsciously take this on themselves as it's all the trash of all the family or even the whole collective globally if this will be put by force onto the innocent – as an abuse. Collective abuse then involves all the systems in it, organisations, institutions, and any forms of cult/community/group/foundation/association. Collective also involves nations from based in one or more countries. If we talk about strategic sadistic abuse, there is something like 'blindness' in the victim (as it is from behind and is not seen obviously) and the more this is done as a sadistic backstab, the worse it is. The victim's blindness comes from the loss of orientation to what is happening behind their back – and remember – you cannot have orientation if it's planned by someone else and it's behind your back! The more the victim is destabilised, the more the victim becomes disorganised. The victim can look for confirmation of what happened to them, and look for the information on why it happened or what happened, and beg the sadist about the current conditions and what they can do a different way. The victim will not go away because the victim has no idea what did really happen behind their back and when was backstabbed in prolongation – this can last all the victim's life or half of their life till victim's tragedy – or death or serious harm as serious victim's disability or lifelong illness. I was backstabbed from early childhood, till the place of healing for several years. After this I removed me to zero from all possible sadists in my life. The victim is drawn to this sadistic dance unconsciously. It's not a dance of sadist and masochist. It's a dance of sadists and the innocent victim who is not even informed that it's a sadistic dance (it's not masochism in the victim – the victim does not know what is happening, it's not a front plate for the victim, it's a backstab). All the games of the sadists were in my life always from the place of the backstab on me and from the place of zero orientation about what was happening.

Sadists will also lie about the victim, and the victim does not have a chance to say anything/or even lie about the sadists as it's happening mainly behind the victim's back. So they try constantly to protect their sadistic false outside image, and they go into sadistic revenge with maliciousness, nastiness and cruelty before the victim is even prepared to act (the victim doesn't know what is happening) – mostly, it's done to the victim who is entirely unarmed and is in open wounds (for example open traumatisation) after sadistic attack; let's say as a form of false public accusations. It's almost like sizzling insects, which are lower than animals because the most significant thing is in an exposition of the victim. These sizzling insects can publicly create malicious perversity about the victim, who is never aware of what is behind their back. One of the strategies is to symbolically "break the spine of the innocent one."

For example, when there is a sadist and a child – so if the

sadist/s will beat the child for the whole game – it's not winning, and it's not the child's fall down. It's a backstab, and the battle is never ever equal. There is never a winner until the victim gets out from this alive – then the only winner is the alive victim. Remember this. When there is a backstab – the innocent doesn't know and is unaware of what truly happened. If the sadists say about the victim, let's say, "now you did fall down" – it's also never a fall down of the innocent one (it's a fall down of the sadists). Again there is no battle at all – it's an invasion and drastic degradation of an unarmed innocent one from behind – it's a loss and true fall down of the sadists. Sadists' victim cannot fall down, as well as, for example, a small kitten who is crying, hiding behind the building as its eyes were gouged out didn't fall down. Think, who did fall down to be so sadistic to gouge out the kitten's eyes? No, this kitten did not fall down. The one who did this to the kitten fell down.

The only loser is always the sadist who is raising on the innocence's harm. The same explanation is about being called an idiot because the sadists did attack from behind and did backstab without the victim's awareness. If, for example, a woman is raped from behind – she is "raped" – taken with force without consent "from behind" – backstabbed. Upon this simple example – who is the loser here and who is the victim? Is this a real war on one unarmed woman without preparation and awareness of what is going on, and she is not aware, the more she is forced? No, it's not a war. It's a group / collective loser (against one innocent) who is falling down while crossing the boundaries of this innocent – and it's not a win, it's a crime.

So we have to see that the sadist has no power to come to the victim as an equal and, let's say, resolve something like an equal. Sadists need power over to release their sadism. It's oppression towards the innocent who is experiencing this oppression from the place where everything is a trap. While on the other hand, the sadist is strategically planning it. The victim is in a full trap. And when the victim is entrapped, then the sadistic perpetrator can do everything. The sadist will use, abuse and take everything from the victim and then when it is done, "move on" to the next victim. The previous victim probably is dead, killed or committed suicide. If the previous victim is still alive, well... they will be kept fully and tremendously on any possible level used until they are thrown away. However, after this, they will be still kept under control that will not come back from the place of removal, for example, the previous marketplace area.

This exact strategy of entrapment and usage of the victim is happening also under kidnapping and this what exactly happened to me when I was kidnapped twice. There is no way out. The entrapped victim has no move-out and cannot "move on."

Planned Sadism with Hidden Agenda

Sadists plan abuse and usage of the innocent. They do plan it, and it's almost like their nature as their every move is based on hidden agenda – profit on the innocent one – based on survival: financial, professional, personal, rising on the innocent, to make from someone a public victim so that they are not the victim themselves, etc. Because sadists plan everything, they also assume that the innocent person also plans everything against the sadists. Sadists plan to backstab because they are scared to be backstabbed. Sadists are scared of the truth about themselves, so they lie about the other person, exposing the other person as a liar who is lying to society – why? Because the sadists lie about themselves, as well as about the others! Sadists are scared of any exposure, mostly public ones, as it's about their fake reputation and exposing themselves, which is why they will expose the innocent one in order to mislead the whole sadistic society. For the sadists, the more drama and the more scandal, the more intensity, the more the sadists feel their grandiose pumps which can lead to the ongoing sadistic inner cycles – they do this consciously or unconsciously (as sadistic collective unconscious).

Let's look at relational examples. There is no cheating if the person is not in a committed relationship. If a marriage is falling apart, it is not because of an external object like a tree on the road, a child's illness or because the dog barked too loud. Marriage is falling apart because two people don't love each other anymore; because of the struggles they are experiencing on the survival level of who they are as a part of growing in life; and also because marriage was set up not from the soul level but rather a human level (for example, construct of cultural/historical settings). A mother who is ill and goes to the hospital or on healing is not leaving her kids because she does not love them. This mother, on healing, heals herself to be WITH and FOR her kids, and she heals because she loves them so much. These two examples can show a woman in a falling apart marriage or a woman in illness can be shown by sadists in a propaganda way as being a cheater or a 'slut on healing' or even both if sadistic slander requires this more... Propaganda suits sadists well as they can manipulate the arena from their grandiose position and repeat their own inner sadistic cycles, so needed for sadists to rise and exist.

Sadists' agenda is based on hatred, and hatred is not human evolution (it's frankly human regression). Why then are false accusations created towards innocence? If there were no agenda, why would false accusations be created by sadists towards the innocent? After all, an innocent person, being a sadist's victim, wants justice. Sadists also want "justice," but their justice is based on power over, and sadistic power to use and abuse. But whom do they want to use and abuse? Sadists, if they want justice, want it mainly from those who were in their past. But for sadists the past is now. So they use, abuse and take "justice" from the innocent people because it's an effortless prey for them. Sadists do not recognize that the innocent one is an absolutely innocent one and has nothing to do with the past predator of the sadists. Sadists do not recognize the person now standing in front of them as sadists are not capable of being in NOW (it's 'doing' without identity). Now, the one who stands in front of the sadist is made by the sadists, the one who belongs to the sadist's past (even the innocent one was not in their past!). Sadists will not address pain towards their original predators as sadists also have predators from the past. In contrast, sadists will address their jealousy and envy towards the innocent one – can you imagine? "About 'me', without me" – as it's only an object of false accusations (object – it can be a plastic block – but they make an object a human!). For me personally it was very surprising to hear that everybody has an agenda just like that, by living on this planet! (and moreover towards me!?) – that people do not connect from the place of connection but from the place of usage and hidden agenda! Truly scary and very, very sad for all humanity! It's like when I heard 2.5 years ago that people don't meet normally. They only meet for profit – they meet with each other because of a hidden agenda! And now imagine, what if the hidden agenda is sadism!? As it was exactly in my case throughout my entire life.

Sadists have agenda under, and the main reason to be around the other or with the other will be a usage – with sadists it will be a sadistic usage. So if let's say lies destroyed my life by people I met 35, 30, 25 or 20 or even 2 years ago, what sort of stories do these people tell? What kind of stories do these people see in their own (sadistic) eyes which are related to the being 20 years ago towards what does not exist anymore on this planet because of my 18 years long transformation, and yes, they are still the same – programmed past points stuck in a timeline somewhere they don't even know where. They are still the same if they have never taken a chance to transform themselves from the inside out. And such people, if have power over, did come and destroy my life, and they will do the same with your life. They backstab Ewa, who they see, let's say, 20 years ago – as they don't see inside, they only see their own first layer – sadistic eyes of the beholder are shown now, for example, on social media.

The scapegoat is treated as a tool – to be released on, while the scapegoat hits the worldwide scapegoat level – from micro to macro level. We have to know that, maybe except in some circumstances, and by my own past experience, a scapegoat is always innocent as the child in a family system is innocent (*I Will Tell, Anyway!* by Ewa Lawresh). That means an innocent child is conditioned to be a sadist's victim and subconsciously will repeat it as an adult if the circumstances and people form the exact occasion. An incest victim is very easily hooked into it if the childhood sadistic experiences created a sadistic dynamic for the child. All this is built on the subconscious level of the innocent of repeating this constantly, and in my circumstances from almost anyone I have ever met in my life; family, friends, teachers, workers, co-workers, bosses, therapists, cults' leaders, any groups, communities, whole countries and including absolutely total strangers.

Sadistic extremism is inside of the sadists, and with this extremism, the sadist will try to input onto the victim to feel release. Let's see the example of two different incest victims. One woman in her psychopathy and sociopathy was in her childhood in a place between her own mother and her own father. Father was in a relationship with her, and she was competing with her own mother for the father's love from the incest perspective while also sleeping with her own sibling. Now she, as an adult, steps into any pair combination where there is a man and a woman, and she repeats this configuration again and again. She wants to compete with the wife for her husband to get him for herself. Every incest is different, now, let's see me stepping there. I am also an incest victim, and I am in a configuration between two adults as I was between two adults in my own childhood. I do not compete for him. He treats me as his child, not a lover. The first incest will pathologically project the sexual relationship while there is no sexual relationship in my case – so look how different is the perspective of two incests as every trauma is different and no trauma can be put as every pancake made with hands prepared on the plate is different – done of course the traditional way. Incest victims are done in the traditional way – each differently.

My life was destroyed by sadists, for me personally, with no clue about it. It's a fact. Why my life was destroyed? Because of the sadists' sadistic attachment to the cult figure as a parental figure.

I am definitely not your mother who abused you – you sadists. I am not your sister who abused you – you sadists. I am not your father who abused you – you sadists. I am not your brother who abused you – you sadists. I am not your

31

teacher who abused you – you sadists. I am not your wife who abused you – you sadists. I am not your husband who abused you – you sadists.

Sadists poured on me their hatred, but this should be not towards me. They all made me their personal, professional, community and society trash bin. Sadists do not treat humans as human. They treat humans as a trash bin, a plastic or metal bin where it is possible to throw everything stuck in them anyway. Sadistic strategic abuse is based on the sadist's amusement. The more excitement the sadist feels from their own inflicted pain onto the innocent one, the more power over the sadist gains inside. It's about toxic sadistic energy in the nervous system of the sadist. So the bigger the sadistic show, the bigger the sadistic exposition, the more excitement sadists feel. Please remember that the innocent one is the healthiest among the sadists. The innocent one fights for survival and naturally is in survival – the innocent do everything to be alive. Sadists never see "human" in the innocent human. Sadists see in the perpetrators the same as themselves as "humans" they see. For them, it's their normal. For the innocence and vulnerability are not normal – such people land in psychiatric hospitals while all the world is one huge psychiatric hospital with the mass disconnected from true feelings, kindness and authenticity. It's important to remember that experiences in childhood are a reflection later in life, unfortunately again on a relational level from the programs created during the ages of 0-7 years old. And it will repeat by itself until the person wilfully heals and transforms from the inside out, which is step by step layout in my authorship program, The Path To Epic Hello (pathtoepichello.com). The program involves coming back to yourself from past programs to NOW through a transformation from inside out and resolving the stress/hormonal level of relational level with sadists in your life (including any pathology such as narcissism, psychopathy, sociopathy, etc.). Stress is interwind from childhood, which creates addiction towards dependency (and as an addiction to dependency) in the nervous system – addicted for the matter of the repetition of unwanted sadism from the others what is step by step also layout in my book, *I Will Tell, Anyway! Games of the First Sadist.* Sadism is happening on a relational level – this for sure. The relational level can reach all over the globe. Sadists are observing and looking for the innocent who will take the scapegoat role and become sadist's victims not only one on one – but they will be a victim even as a collective victim of sadism.

Confusion

Sadists cannot stay with confusion. Sadists think that they have full ownership of an innocent person. It's the main characteristic that they think, they lead your life for the innocent one that they refuse to give to the innocent one human rights of CHOICE – sadists will do everything to prove they are right as they "know what you think" inside of your head as an innocent one and also they are sure "what your intentions are" in every single possible life situation and in every behaviour of the innocent one.

Sadists will destroy an innocent person because of feeling inner confusion, so they have to stay sure of what the innocent person is doing and saying and even thinking. Sadists are capable of killing innocent ones to prove that the sadists were right. Sadists have to be right mostly publicly as all others are watching them – a sadistic image is the most important, and it's all a form of extremism. Sadists believe in their rightness and their fake accusations toward the innocent one to the extent that they even kill for their beliefs. Again – it's a form of extremism – in most cases expressed through hissed rage propaganda and slander smear campaigns.

A scapegoat is the one on whom all is poured and released. Innocence is not a passage of release. The release should happen not through innocence but through the sadistic self inside the sadist – in the exact body beholder. But sadists make innocence their tool for this.

As the example of this is when let's say, the girl is running and falls down and scrapes her knee, and she sees the blood. She starts crying and calling, "Mum, mum, I hurt myself." A sadist's response will be an attack on the child rather than love, care, compassion, and understanding. Unfortunately, a sadist is not capable of such traits, neither keeping the child in positive regard nor loving the child just by their existence. The sadist from this place will punish the child for the blood on the knee and inflict even more pain on the child as the sadist feels empowered from the place of the power over and control of the situation. The sadist wants not what is the child's need – the release of sadism is happening at the same time as the advantage on the child in these circumstances. It's inhuman and almost hard to believe that a human can act this way towards the innocent one.

The child is blamed for the effect of what happened to them. Sadistic blame is based on this. In the same way, the traumatised person – an innocent one – is blamed for their reactive state, where this is a very natural trauma response to dealing with trauma for the traumatised innocent. The person is "hysterical" under CIA interrogation trials – yes, of course, is "hysterical." What would you expect from a traumatised, innocent human?

So sadistic strategic abuse is based on pouring onto the vulnerable person to degrade the innocent one and for sure never ever up level. The main agenda for the sadists is inflicting punishment for the one who, in fact, is in need because is under trauma. Sadists will punish the innocent one for the inflicted trauma and then will punish for the effects of more drastic traumatisation in the innocent. Then will undermine, for example, the innocent person's motherhood – while the innocent one is already traumatised to the level of barely breathing (now sadists can judge whatever they want and prosecute about whatever they want, even for example, because of not the exact facial expression the sadists wish the innocent has on their face or such ridiculousness like the eyebrows of the victim are too small, too wide or too narrow, whatever) – in here – this way my whole motherhood was undermined – and by WHOM? By sadists. We do not speak here about neediness from a place of unresolved attachment; remember – a sadist will use it for the reactivation states in the innocent to prove that, let's say, their motherhood is bad. If we open our eyes to this kind of abuse, we can see which way abusive, sadistic systems are created. Institutional regime around parenthood of innocent people who do everything they can to be alive for their kids. Let's see this closer on my example. I was travelling the world to heal myself from childhood and early attachment wounds, so my focus was on the earliest levels of human development (0-7 years old) and what as a finished effect is shown in my published book, *I Will Tell, Anyway!* To achieve this kind of healing, I was looking for myself. I mainly focused on my childhood and being a target of emotional, physical and mostly sexual abuse. The working process of healing this particular matter lasted from 2016-2021 (2016 – my first trip to Australia to heal early attachment wounds; 2017 – a second trip to Australia, next stage of healing; 2020 – 7 years after my father's death, and the first time visiting his grave to make a closure for me; 2021 – a published book about what inhibited in me as a subconscious terror and threat – and that I will tell about it, anyway). In my case, early attachment wounds healing included incest healing, so mainly, I was focused on healing sexual wounds. I was not 'travelling' as a "slut" (how sadists behind my back talked about me) to experience sexual intercourse. I was travelling to heal everything possible that happened to me in my childhood (including being kidnapped and dragged by my perpetrator who made a financial profit on me with his 'monkeys'). For the observers, Ewa was a "prostitute" based on the observers' repressed sexual paranoia desires, projections and observers' inner regime mixed with the inner oppressor and inner harasser. For Ewa – Ewa was doing the most sacred work possible for herself – healing early developmental stages, including sexual wounds, incest and being kidnapped. And she healed all the wounds through all these years. Sadists call Ewa a "prostitute" today, and she is at home now. Sadists will turn everything upside down what the innocent one is doing. And they lie. External image is what matters to them. Truth? Who cares?

Which way do they turn the "image" upside down? I go for natural skin treatment, go out from the cabinet with a red face as the effect of the treatment – sadists will turn upside down to use the red face for toxic shame and revenge. I travel to heal myself, and naturally, I cry a lot for what happened to me in my childhood grieving, sadists will turn it upside down and accuse me falsely that I left the kids and am attending parties now. I draw a picture and naturally take my tongue out to be more focused, what children normally do, and the sadist will turn it upside down that I am turning him on, and he will abuse me now sadistically (*I Will Tell, Anyway!* by Ewa Lawresh). I am better at healing than most people older than me in the same market, so to remove me from the market where healing involves using hands as support in treatment – sadists will accuse me of "prostitution." Isn't that – sadistically 'smart' false accusation? Removing someone from the market is very easy – and no, there was no harassment in Australia.

When sadistic strategic abuse happens, you have to see both – the victim and the sadists' abuse. Where are sadists now, and where are innocent people now? After all. Sadists act in groups – then they feel the most strong. They have bigger power over, as remember – sadists are very small level people who take revenge on innocent kids, on weakened people, on the one who is alone and without defences. The victim is always alone.

Sadists isolate information from the innocent one and also isolate it from the place of hidden agenda. Sadists use innocence for their own agenda – they build all careers on the innocent one and all their lives, while the innocent one is left fully used, abused and exploited for free.

Chapter 3

How Strategic Sadism
Removes HER From the Map

3

Motherhood as a Trash Bin

*M*otherhood – is not based on the expectations of the sadistic inner punitive mother in hatred. Judged motherhood is a judged kid who is pregnant in most cases with the kid and is thinking about their mommy who is a kid. Healthy motherhood is not patriarchate motherhood, it's something different. Motherhood beyond sadistic illusions – rooted motherhood I was fighting for.

Patriarchate trash is put onto motherhood as to blame anyone in patriarchate is a place to blame a mom and the way she does her motherhood. Everyone knows how to be a mom, while every child from any generation is a representation of addictions and disconnection. But they know, mostly when the one who does not have kids, they also know. They all know... even men who have never been pregnant, they also know. All know, only the mom does not know... no, she does not know anything – she is a general 'idiot' – and even she knows something about motherhood, she still does not know... Why? Because it's a sadistic system – sadist 'knows' better how to be a mom, no matter who the speaker is now. But in fact, in the patriarchate, they know better how to 'do' moms – by encaging a woman (now they will take everything from her and leave her only with kids, now a human on two legs is under control the next 25 years of their life) – all is done by force and all is done by patriarchate system – a production of controlled house-caged parent.

Mom, who did not make a career because of her motherhood and is in hatred because of jealousy and 'lost' past, will from a place of authority or the majority of same "losers" – force other innocent mom to live under her beliefs (lost 'past' – "I was living this way and you will live this way"... wow!) but not under innocent mom's beliefs (What is that? Now we have one slave of beliefs who is forcing like under rape – to become the next slave of these beliefs). Remember, patriarchate motherhood is about 'doing,' and they do not distinguish it, just as sadists do not distinguish 'doing' from 'being.' Sadists do not know how to 'be.'

Now we have a war of beliefs ("losers" in a place of authority and innocent moms)! Sadists catch a piece of meat – an innocent mom – and they surround her like attacking hyenas. And they will do what they want and about, and with innocent woman's motherhood', because they all 'know'!

Sadistic persecutors (single sadists or sadistic communities as one sadistic social justice including sadistic social workers who treat positions as a place of release on innocent) will judge the innocent mom who, in fact, is doing everything for her happiness and that of her own children that she will be judged by sadists "a selfish one" even as she fights for her kids' and her own freedom. Please remember I am speaking here about an innocent mom, not a sadistic mom, aka "sick monster." Sadists will make her a monster – a mother (sometimes even a 'man') – who needs to be fired on the stake (so that sadists can finally release their hatred) – for the sake of the mothers of the sadists. These are sadists who are ashamed of their motherhood and feel guilt towards the motherhood of their mothers and the motherhood of their own – this is a core place of sadistic burning!

Sadists will input all negative projections towards the innocent mom and turn upside down any higher actions that innocent mother does – for the matter of the voice of the sadists because they are the majority and they are on the fake reputation/authority place. Sadists decide now – they are ashamed of their own motherhood, and now they speak, and now they decide – no, you mother, you are ugly (because "my mother was ugly"/"I was ugly in motherhood"), and you are a selfish mom (because "my mom was selfish"/"I was selfish in motherhood"), and you are exploiting and tormenting me [or your own kids!] (because "my mom was exploiting and tormenting me being a kid"/"I was doing it towards my own kids"). Well, sadists – it's your inner disgracefulness and disgust to be a mother yourself, your inner shame of motherhood, and your hatred towards motherhood. It's your inner torment when you torment an innocent mom of two, exploiting her publicly worldwide... more in total, it's a case to the Supreme Court!

Sadists who have never had children and have never been a parent will be the most lauded in this – they are lauded subconsciously for their own mommy-hatred reasons. Unfortunately, who gave them the voice in a place they should never have one? Sadists are limited in their smallness and mindset to such an extent that they will falsely accuse a mom of anything drastically possible – first, they accuse falsely only because she exists! (and unfortunately remains for them their own mom (aka 'sick monster') or their own motherhood (aka 'guilt monster')). The most unfair place of judgement and blame and sadistic public persecution was a place – for them (and why for them?) – my own motherhood. It was all shown through the eyes of sadistic beholders.

Work Area (sadistic jealousy has no end) – How Easily to Remove Her

The sadistic person will attract innocence first and try to charge on the innocence to destroy them, mainly for a better position and public face. And the sadist is always like a parasite in there with their own toxicity in their sadistic mind. From their sadistic mind, they act – unfortunately – upon their own sadistic mind. This same is happening in all sadistic communities that carry ONE sadistic mind, and they act upon or individually or as a group upon an innocent one – a created scapegoat. Sadists feel more power when they act with two or more together. They then as well as in a sadistic family system – destroy the innocent one as the community member to up level community so that now the community looks better on the outside. For the one community member destroyed publicly is somehow lightening up that sadistic community as ONE looks better publicly than ever before. Can you imagine? And also this way the competition works between them! They removed the best one – always the most hard-working/talented innocent – for the matter of profiting on this person rather than on any other. Sadistic strategic abuse is based on competition that sadistic competitors will do everything to win over the innocent one through constant disruptions inflicted on the innocent person's life. It's not moral and is not based on any ethics. So this is a human without humanity, who is hidden with all actions based on usage of the other to achieve anything in life on the innocence – mostly money and positions to gain power over. All sadistic family and sadistic institutional systems are based on denial of their own sexuality, and it's a collective subconscious. All actions of sadists are based on usage, they are not based on love, as love is not a usage. Sadism is in fact a 'non-relational way' of doing things in life, and absolutely not based on connection, presence and safety. This dance is between sadists and the victim to gain something over the victim. Sadistic slut shaming (paradoxically and for women and for men) is one of the most used tools by sadists. Sadistic perverts are hidden behind sadistic patriarchate culture and are gaining this perverse control over the victim's sexuality (whatever sex, this only needs to be a scapegoat – the one who fits is mostly the one who was sexually on physical level abused in childhood – in a severe, raw, harsh, intense, drastic, sore way in prolongation) and abuse of the power they have currently and wish to gain over this power over the victim. If an innocent person is not a 'slut' will become one (will be made by sadists), no proof (will be invented, don't worry) – not clear (will be retouched, don't worry). It's happening everywhere and mainly in the business area where there is the highest competition among people in women's bodies (at least it was exactly in my case). Remember – if your business is attractive to the sadists – they will do everything to remove you from the market – they will remove you and take your business and your knowledge – in most cases putting their own name there. It's a crime.

Sadism is like malicious cancer, which is trying to slowly spread in any direction onto the victim and their life step by step. And this malicious cancer has to be cut off entirely so that the victim survives and has a safe space for healing, raising and adjusting to what happened to them (in fact, what was done to them behind their back). The victim in this place needs to digest everything, heal the wounding and let it go. Sadistic strategic abuse is always planned and is based on market/financial (money) power over (even me being kidnapped was based on this). And if there is any opportunity that their hate can be released, the sadistic perpetrator will do this. Their hatred is based on repressed sadistic, never processed, squeezed sexuality.

Shame is a powerful tool for sadists as they are full of inner shame and contempt. So they strategically prepare how and which steps to use to remove the victim from the market – amongst women is mainly used a sadistic tool: "slut shaming" – mostly from women against women; amongst men is used a sadistic tool: "harassment shaming" – mostly from women against men. Anyone who is slut shaming has an inner slut or is not resolved, and not released. The same accordingly is happening with a tool: harassment. Anyone who is harassment shaming has an inner harasser or is not resolved, and not released. Maybe sadists' inner slut needs to resolve it this way but is doing this through the innocent person (which is a crime). And again in here, the same is with harassment. Maybe the sadists' inner harasser needs to resolve it this way but is doing this through the innocent one (which is a crime and more over does not lead to any healing for the sadist).

Steps are very easy – they try to attack again and again, and it's like a malicious parasite – it's almost like innocent, vulnerable people need to isolate themselves from sadistic parasites and take a love vaccine to heal the wounds and all scars inflicted on them from strategic sadistic abuse. Sadists, from their smallness, while using titles, positions and reputation, use fake power over with traumatised (by them) innocence now, who is being on reactions after traumatisation. Sadists attack as predators from their smallness based on toxic shame and jealousy. So for example sadists will mix healthy looking face for the matter of red face – healthy looking face has a child in their aliveness – red face is connected with shamed sexuality through sexual abuse on the child! (*I Will Tell Anyway!* by Ewa Lawresh). In fact, the sadist is always smaller than the victim and is on the most lower level and evolution and existence. That is why sadists backstab like insects without consent on and on and like an animal from behind, attacking or biting from maliciousness. Sadists never speak face to face like human – human in the communication based on reciprocity and understanding. NEVER. Sadists gossip behind your back from the game of "Chinese whisperers" mentioned below. You can ask for a talk and loving kindness and being genuine in this, but you will never receive it. The level of human talk as reciprocity is not part of a sadistic tool and is not part of the usage. Let's see this closer.

How Institutional, Community and Societal Madness Removes HER From the Map

My life was destroyed by other people's thoughts which created in themselves judgments about who I am as their own sadistic projections. Sadistic judgements created in a group rumours on a level of "Chinese whispers" – a children's game which is based on first, in this case, sadistic judgement, but the repetition of transformed sadistic judgement creates the ripple effect of the false wave of sadistic massive thoughts. So the sadist needs to start from themselves. Sadists' self is disturbed by sadism so that there is no authentic self in the sadists. Instead, there is only a pile of false constructs in their rigid pathological mind (rather *wild*) out of any embodiment. From now on, there are only sadistic judgements.

People who believe in something popping out as a thought, which does not exist here and now, see only things that exist in their own heads. It's not connected with factual things, mostly if something happened an hour ago, a few days ago, or back even 20 years ago. So how can we find the truth in this? The thoughts come and go, they travel in the head constantly. The more sick and rigid mind (rather *wild*) on cultural differences and diversity, the sicker, psychopathic and sadistic will be their minds and eyes of their beholders and then, unfortunately, the actions that follow their sick minds. Thoughts are in a sadistic person triggered and connected with them inside – this is what is in the sadistic mind, it's not in the outside reality. If somebody feels, let's say, anxious, that is a part, for example, of the marginalised group or minority in a society can have a certain package of thoughts based on inner hatred which will be projected to destroy the innocent one – unfortunately, the one who even can be on their side protecting or fighting for diversity rights. If anyone feels shamed they will have a certain package of thoughts based on shame. If a sadistic group believes that a judgemental day will come for them, in that case, they will choose an innocent scapegoat to put this all as a judgemental day onto this person – it's part of imaginary in their own head (paranoia) – let's say "armageddon" as the last judgement. It has nothing to do with an open heart and humanity in a human or more, in the whole community, who is as a collective in survival, because of beliefs about the punishment day from the one in whom they believe. They will put the same amount of punishment onto the innocent one – their object of sadistic relief – their scapegoat.

Collective chatterbox from past programs is a dangerous mixture of social media or general talk therapy madness sadistic communities nowadays. The triggered person cannot just like that step back from themselves, go out from themselves where they are in survival, they cannot leave their survival. Their judgement comes from the defensive mechanisms, so they pour all possible negativity (conscious/unconscious, hidden negativity and repression all inside of the sadistic beholder) onto the scapegoat – but never ever on themselves. The collective now form one – is spreading onto all of them with more and more madness (therapy sadistic communities madness can be again pointed towards the innocent scapegoat making this scapegoat mad – it's sadism). As a group, you will never see the truth – you have to separate yourself from the sickness of sadistic communities. Communities are sicker than one single, separated person as forming a 'war' one on one (please remember this one!). Community madness spreads twisted fogginess, and all turn into a children's blame-sadism-game level where adults in the high positions with enormous power over use their sadistic voice. From now on, they are now not even playing but living the Chinese whisperer's game while a message is a whisper from one ear towards the other ear. It's not professional and lacks basic tools – ethics, morals and healthy boundaries. People lose lives because of these thoughts (transported onto outside sentences) ear to ear messages – this is dangerous!

- "I bought a cable at the market."
- "She bought the cable at the market."
- "She bought the cat at the market."
- "She bought the Kate at the Mark's place."
- "She is a whore who is paying Mark to sleep with Kate."
- "Kate is a whore who is with Mark."
- "Kate is a lesbian who does not like Mark."
- "Mark said that he doesn't know Kate."
- "Mark said that he is a lesbian who doesn't know Kate."
- "Mark and Kate are not lesbians as Mark is a man."
- "Mark is a man, and now he is thinking to become Kate."

We can listen to these stories based on the variations of the modality constructs of the other person mind / sickness / illusions / madness / disorders / hatred / jealousy / envy / revenge / pathology / psychopathy / sociopathy / internalised phobias (in this case from the sadists' perspective). The more the person is sadistic and the more personal connection is with or the recipient of the sentence, hidden agenda of the impression or hatred towards cables, markets, cats, people named Kate, Mark, LGBTQ+, men, women, phobias, or even the world just in general... sadism then has no end, and the hissed creativity under sadism either. Can you imagine?

So let's check here the first and the last ear to ear message: "I bought a cable at the market." = "Mark is a man, and now he is thinking to become Kate." So now, where is the reality and where is the sick mind, and where is the sadistic revenge (prejudice, ambiguity, confusion based on inner fears/phobias of the sadists based on any form of bias) and mostly NOW? If this is met within a cultural regime or within a 'rapistic' sadistic community where beliefs are rigid (rather *wild*) and based on extremes, or even to the narcissist ego within a group or community as one sadistic ego: "I bought the cable at the market." = "Mark is a man, and now he is thinking to become Kate." we can start thinking if there is a preparation for the third war on this planet. More some sadistically rigid (including therapy field, belief field, etc.) communities (rather *wild* so also aligned with nature rather extremes of rigidity) will kill (literally), or there will be an attempt to kill (literally) – so to such extend that… These are only sentences… only sentences… and only sentences… (words in some combinations – that's all!) based on somebodies' thoughts in their own head! Sadists do not recognise sentences under creative writing in them or others (let's say my creative notebooks) and reality – as gossip is a form of addiction in sadistic people as well as control (they need special institutionalisation for getting out from addictions to gossip and controlism). Think now – sentences above as "Chinese whispers" are said by whom? In this simple example, we have 11 sentences – can I ask you to play for a moment? Can you play with different people who say these sentences? Different people can be let say: two known actors, two people with an internalised phobia about being a Lady, two people who are sellers on the market, two people under trauma, two people who plan to ruin somebodies life because they feel jealousy and cannot control this simple emotion, two people who are in greed and will never ever give back the money they owe even they signed the agreements to pay it back, two kids, two teens, a pair who is planning to rob a bank, two therapists in sadistic hatred, two mad psychologists out of humanity, two self-made millionaires, two older women professors at the university who hatred themselves and both of them lost partners in various situations, two people who are sitting in a cafe after party, two women who hatred towards their colleague, etc. These are just examples. Now let's combine the mass... not two speakers-gossipers – now let's combine the mass, how about when we combine sadistic mass? (as this what happened in my case). And now, from face to face talk, let's move to social media talks... this place is a place of pouring all the animal sadistic hissing – from the sadistic subconscious. Remember – in this place am asking all the social systems, including social organisations, to STOP this mass hysteria, that they STOP themselves and withhold steps in reality as in this place, we have no longer reality (only sadism in my case). There was never reality and will never be reality. We have already lost too many innocent people on this planet because of sadistic madness, including Ladies.

What is the tool of the sadist that the sadist has this power over? So it's not only certain public position, reputation and titles. These are also supportive 'connections' from sadists' communities. Sadist takes their own inner etiquette, which describes the sadist and put it onto the victim. So let's say, for example, the sadist uses some information from the past of the victim which can be manipulated – so transported information from the past onto the present time which naturally is not connected with the victim in many cases and even with the present time of the sadists and the sadistic receivers. So, for example, sadists to remove someone from a job which involves working with kids will falsely accuse the victim, for example, of harassment (or any other sex related topic – remember) – as a form of slut shaming/harassment shaming – just to put attention towards some kind of relational crimes – while sadist is the one who is abusing kids in this instance themselves.

Let's see this closer. I am not an alcoholic although I was in a place for addiction treatment and only working on my relationship with primal caregivers. This information of me being in the treatment centre gives the sadists to use this information to influence if I can be on the certain working market or not, if I am a good mother or not, if I am after my motherhood or I am after earning money leaving my kids with the others – so the ugly judgement has no end. The person who asked me to sign the paper on the mentioned addictions treatment said to me, "Can you sign this document; otherwise, I cannot offer you the treatment for free", and there was a place on the document which showed that I am an alcoholic after signing it. I had never had issues to be in a psychiatric hospital. I was there for 3 nights as there was no place to put me safely elsewhere to wait to transport me to the mentioned treatment centre. For the sadists, any situation can be used for the sadistic analysis to drag out any information from my life to prosecute me publicly and make it the way that the audience believes in what wants to believe (for the show matters, for the laughing at matters) – mostly in their own internal judgement about their own blaming self-motherhood and addictions. What is fascinating is that the truth is coming out through what the sadists accuse you as an abyss between their sadistic mind and who the innocent person is. The bigger point in this is to destroy somebody's reputation.

Remember – sadists justify their guilt by the chosen scapegoat's life – that's why they are destroying an innocent person's life/motherhood/womanhood/innocence, etc.:

- And no, the guilt of the sadist about their motherhood is not the guilt of the innocent one about their motherhood.
- And no, the guilt of the sadists about their womanhood morals is not the guilt of the innocent one about their womanhood morals.
- And no, the guilt of the sadists about their destruction of the other person's innocence, it's not guilt of the innocent one about their lost innocence because of the sadists.

Next examples: I was never a drug addict, but I met many people who were and even was in short relationships with some in my past. I was never diagnosed on any level of any mental illness, while sadists and sadistic communities diagnosed me on distance (if you see the diagnosis about me anywhere, it's a crime as a diagnosis on distance are already against the rules of any professional psychological association and are not ethical and never ever true) many

many times by negative projections and their own insecurities, fears and moreover hidden agendas to reach their own aims on the market. I heard many things 'about me' – and in fact not about me – from the project "About 'me', without me" so "About Ewa without Ewa" – that Ewa was stealing cars, Ewa was never paying anyone, etc. It's slander – a sadists' smear campaign – observe this publicly clearly – they already did shoot themselves in the foot! The judging me from their eyes of sadistic beholder perspective (who are in here therapeutic societies who in this case exactly shoot themselves in the foot – if you find any of it anywhere about me) with no facts, from false assumptions and false accusations.

So how the message is turned upside down? I was globally promoting mental health and well–being as I find mental health is one of the most important health we should take care of and my inner calling supported this message. No, I was not promoting mental illness. How far the message can be turned upside down...? So this way, sadists create public information about the targeted object. I was promoting to feel the feelings while the message was turned upside down. No, I was not promoting prostitution, abandoned kids, and party girl. I was promoting feeling the feelings that support mentioned above mental health and well – being so in this, I was promoting healthy, safe love, connection with kids and centred woman in inner stillness through self-empowerment from inside out. Isn't this surprising how far the sadists can turn it upside down, frankly, in the end, showing their true faces who they are?

While I was healing early attachment wounds, including wounds from childhood sexual abuse, I was shown as an idiot while I was frankly doing the most sacred work possible for me to be healthy and happy and be a mother I have never had through re-parenting me. This process publicly was named – that I am an idiot. Is that truly idiotic to heal yourself for the matter of better life and parenting and for the better life of my 2 kids I love so much? Is an idiot a person who heals herself because she was raised in a sadistic, abusive family among sadistic systems and sadistic societies? (*I Will Tell, Anyway!* by Ewa Lawresh).

The sadistic community that is slut shaming again is a slut in shame fully as a sadistic community themselves – a community repressed entirely with hidden sluts and harassers interwind in one sadism. And sadist who is slut shaming the victim – is simply a slut in shame as themselves being the sadist. So we have to understand that this is almost like a sadistic business which is flourishing from sadism and gaining more and more from their victim. And everything is based on shame, punishment, maliciousness, aggression and hatred. There is no compassion (and please never count on healthy, loving and genuine care that there will be one), there is also no understanding as there is only hatred.

Isolation

Isolation narrows your perspective and being controlled narrows the possibilities. How does sadistic isolation look like? I published the book, and I paid for publishing it. I have exclusive rights to my book, *I Will Tell, Anyway! Games of the First Sadist*. There were sold only two books of mine in the English language till today. There has been no sold any Polish language book of mine yet. Sadists will take care not to let you be on the market this or other way. They treat the innocent one as their possession (to put the object into these braces, they will infantilise the woman for this matter through psychological tortures). The traumatised woman goes into the girl position not because she has never grown up but because she is now "hysterical" while CIA experiments are inflicted on her. Have you ever seen how an innocent animal reacts just before being killed? It does not go into freeze, it will be fighting in the reactional level – this is the exact level when the sadists will call a moving 'object' (a woman, let's say under rape) a "whore" and a "slut" – to possess the person again under the institutionalisation matter or any other authority level. This creates the squizzeness publicly in the victim (a "whore" or not a "whore," whatever) who is innocent will go into under inner oppression now even for the matter of unconscious transgenerational trauma – as long as will not start healing process of loving themselves (what of course takes time).

Sadists, the most are scared to lose their object of possession – a human 'pet' which is their supplier and their outside extension. Sadists keep them short on the leash – as they wish never let the object to loosen the leashing line. It's a power over game. They will do everything that the innocent will never grow up and never reach personal and mostly professional independence. Sadists create some kind of exclusivity in it – "You cannot work with anyone else," "You cannot open your own business, as you are working for me," "You cannot talk with random people as you can only talk with me," "You cannot... believe in other believes rather the believes I have," "You cannot spend your motherhood differently than I spent it" – these all justifications and threats are important for the sadists as sadists want to rule.

The next one is: sadists will not take for themselves and will not give to the others – keeping possession (an innocent human on the leash) for themselves it's some kind of asset – sadists shine through the "human asset" but never shine through themselves (as they have a lot to hide). As a reverse, this is tragic when sadists expose negativity about themselves through innocent "human asset" – it's tremendous abuse happening there. This way, kids with special needs are treated in many sadistic families/ institutions, including innocent healthy! patients put by sadists into psychiatric hospitals. So, in fact, we have healthy people who are treated less than animals...

Sadists keep also on a short leash innocent person motherhood... to control HER – mostly her motherhood that she cannot come back on the market, for example (if she wants to come back on the market, the lash out starts to turning her motherhood onto her fatherhood – no one knows WHY?). Sadists don't understand that there is a natural way of motherhood in a healthy person. Motherhood is not a mom and kids where – 2 rooms as 4 walls say 'hello' to each other. Motherhood is not about staying in the building for the next 25 years (even in prison, are better circumstances offered for a single man without kids than this what is offered by patriarchate for a mom staying at home) for a woman who is a HUMAN as well as a man and as well as anyone who has no kids – she is a human – yes, exactly – a mom is a human as well.

Sadistic social justice is the best in this and is hitting all the records about 'motherhood on leash' their own way as a patriarchal way – for this, they can use social persecution towards an innocent one – the scapegoat one – even the scapegoat mom has the best possible intentions ever in this place hitting divine levels. For the patriarchal mindset, it's not in their category of understanding. More, it brings confusion, how come a mom could possibly wish to heal her childhood wounds for herself and her kids and her kid's future... "no, it's impossible, she is a bad mom – attack her!". Now all is justified by the sadistic societies – they are right, and the innocent mom is wrong. "No way, what is she doing? She is supposed to stay at home. This is where is her place!" Well... if she had a 4th stage cancer and she was in a hospital/hospice / if she had a heart operation / if she had a long lasting few years rehabilitation – where kids are limited to visit their parent – well, she/all is then justified... but... mental/trauma healing? Early attachment wounds healing? FOR BETTER MOTHERHOOD??? "Oh NO!" "Let's attack her! Let's hang her! Let's all kill her!" "We have the right!" "She is just a woman, a simple mom of two! Her place are 4 walls!" "No career, for moms!" "You are a pet, your place is where I say your place is, and your place is in 4 walls." "You stay in 4 walls room, and we take your business," "We have a right, you are only a stupid woman, a stupid mom – just an idiot!"

Sadists even acquire that sexual organs of the innocent woman (mom) belong to the sadists... From now on, it's a meat preparation to be put in the slaughterhouse – "Open your legs, now we decide"... It's their meat... you are not your own "meat," it's their meat. It's a "meat" which belongs to sadistic societies (including profit-innocence-usage rising – watch out what was done to me behind my back – what does it look like?). There is no human, and there is no humanity. Sadists do not know what "human" and "humanity" means.

I have seen lastly a short video where the panther was literally dragging dead deer, just hunted and killed, on the top of the tree. Death hunted animal was placed there like a dragged heavy pillow. It looks like the whole dinner is dragged up for the animal to eat the other animal fully in a steady, slow motion way. The panther is possessing now the other – a whole and dead animal. If the animal wasn't dead, would be in freeze while still would be victimised and traumatised. Well... the animals' nature, especially in wildness, is a norm to survive that one animal eats the other one. No, even for a single moment, there is no consideration is that love? Is that hate? Is that contempt? It's just nature. It's animal nature. Human nature is not to eat the other human because the human has to eat, not to die. The human who is vulnerable is though eaten by the sadists...

Strategic sadistic abuse is about possessing the innocent

one fully and ripping the innocent one into pieces until the last piece is left, mostly what is finished by the death of the innocent one. In most cases, though sadists want the innocent to be alive as long as the innocent is bringing the "profit", or you name it... This ripple into pieces is done in a very ritualistic way through the show, scandal, to such extent that the exaggeration and extremes will hit the caricature of accusations, caricature of abuse, caricature of slander/defamations to smash the public face of the innocent one. Sadism is done in a show way and in a hidden way. Some innocent are kidnapped and just disappear forever. Others are in one on one relation where everything (even keeping the money) is on the side of the sadists, but never on the side of the innocent one... The sadist's victim is gradually degraded personally and publicly by toxic lies and false accusations based on tricky agenda. The sadists possess innocence by possessing the victim in their 'hands'. The victim is fully entrapped and then slowly more and more weakened. When the victim is very weak, and trauma is reactivated, this intimidated individual goes into a shock and from this place as being entrapped goes into the freeze and is becoming like the deer on the tree, fully caught, obsessively controlled by the sadists and also fully possessed as an object – tool – to be slowly eaten to zero. This way, many innocent people disappear from the map – to zero. Sadists never wish to give freedom to the person to be themselves. They always wish that the person is who the sadists wish the person is – believe what the sadists believe, see the world the way sadists see and act in the world the way sadists act. It's being a sadist's pet/puppet in a full possible form. Nothing more, nothing less. If the sadists can exploit the victim more, they will do it. As long a "pet" is a "pet" that long, everything is okay. The sadists have complete control over the victim – once the victim is looking for their independence – the revenge starts (REMEMBER) – "What!? You are going away to the other person?" – even the innocent one is going nowhere or is talking with a friend about the next academic lecture, whatever, "it's over! Now I will show you!!!" sadists scream from a distance... The innocent one is controlled on any possible level, including money control, as sadists withhold payments, even sadists signed agreements (many sadists make money on the innocent one while innocent one is not even being informed about this and moreover without any consent what is a crime, btw while innocent one can at the same time live in debts). Not to pay the money back, the sadists will collect with the other sadists, mostly in pairs/triads against the innocent one to not give the innocent one the earned on the innocent money back. It's for them almost like a power game dynamics – they have an agreement on paper, but they will refuse to pay it back. It's based on sadistic greed, so to keep somebodies money for themselves, sadists will invent the next sadistic smear, aka slander campaign (it's a crime), to show their power over the innocent as a form of backstabbing. There will be a refusal of the signed agreement "I will not pay the invoice because till today I paid you more than enough," "You have persecutory beliefs to pay you back, I will not pay the invoice," "You do not take care of my kid, and you wish to take care of your own kids, no, for this I will not pay you the invoice" – can you imagine to be a financial worker in a bank debt department that the person who owes money for the institution, would say such sentences to the worker of the bank for example – that they are refusing to pay the debt back? But such sentences are spoken to the innocent one. The same dynamics – the other attitude. Sadists are fake people with a fear of authority themselves, that is why they love to play authority figures, even if they are nobody, they will play this way on a group level. Then visually, from the outside, they look bigger enough to form one sadist as the whole group/community/society. Innocent one as one has no chances, mainly if the sadists stand behind and stab from behind. And the innocent one at the end hears the sentence from the sadistic backstabber as an explanation for group back-stabbing "No one has never ever harmed me more than you"... justifying their backstab on the innocent. And I would ask you here: "Really, was this me who harmed you in December 1975 or someone else, and you projected this onto my person?" and I had to pay for the other from exactly December 1975 – even though I was not yet born that time.

Entrapped in Submission

Strategic sadistic abuse is based on any kind of torture, the same as under sado-maso / dominant-submission dynamics in a real sexual dynamic based on consent and awareness of mutual maturity! adults! while I speak in this book about mostly psychological tortures which entrap the victim – and everything is without consent. The victim is repeatedly under this entrapment, totally unaware as its indirect sadistic entrapment.

Degradation of the victim is done step by step in a non-consensual way while the victim is not aware and goes under complete submission through enormous vulnerability while at the same time being entrapped. Sadists entrap the innocent by reaching subconsciously to their inner program. They interwind the heat of the moment, and they touch the pressure in the victim by trapping the victim under intimidation. The pressure is risen in the innocent because the innocent is trapped in this situation mostly without any voice like exactly in my case – left alone with activated selective mutism back then, which I experienced most of my life, formed in my childhood based on experienced tortures. At the same time, I was being intimidated and threatened to death place by other sadists and a group of sadists on an ongoing basis. My freedom started when I expressed the trapped voice finally on social media fully – while being proud of my actions – from sadism experienced previously in the competitive field of many business areas in which I was involved back then. My "scream" towards liberation was a "scream" towards my own freedom, which finally I achieved by freeing my voice and my selective mutism as a first step. Sadists are full of sadistic energy inside. They cannot stand this energy consciously or unconsciously, so they are looking for the easy prey they can trap and pour this sadistic energy onto an innocent person. Sadistic strategic abuse is based on a "relational field" of sadistic release. So for the sadists, there has to be a sadistic relational field to release sadistic energy from power over and from the place of control. Sadist is yearning to diminish the victim, the victim on the other hand because is putting so much cost throughout the years, for example, in this relationship, in this workplace area, in this career, or something that is costly of time and/or energy – this all is creating a sadistic bonding with the sadist/s. It's very abusive bonding that, for the innocent victim, is hard even to go away as it is based on conditioning and programming, and in most cases, it's an addictive dynamic until the victim is fully healed.

Chapter 4

Tortures Without Consent

Boundaries

Raping woman boundaries... Sadism is based on violation of human rights and exploitation of the wildness and pureness of the innocence... to the end... Sadists will protect their own ownership and boundaries but will cross the other person's boundaries as soon as possible. Sadists feel their privilege, for this is almost like the sadist is claiming, "I have an intrinsic right to cross your boundaries."

Tortures Without Consent

Once, I had to go immediately into surgery in my teenage years. I was not informed that there would be unwelcomed visitors who would come and investigate my openly spread pussy between my openly spread two legs right when at the moment I was lying on a gynaecological table. And they just arrived. Just like that – tourists, let's say from abroad with their 'cameras' – so Polish learning medical students in my case with their eyes as 'cameras' of penetration beholders –

came and watched me there towards my openly spread two legs and what was between them. I was a teenager, and I was so shy. There was no consent, but offered a full preversy (who can prove there was no sexual arousal in anyone of them? Was I really only an observatory "meat" without consent?). They observed me from my pussy perspective without any permission. I remember this feeling that the nurse was sitting nearby me that she took my hand and whispered to my ear, "Don't look there, everything will be all right," so I turned my head to the side 'disappearing' for the next years or longer... while having contact with her support that time, in the place of public rape not even being asked if I wish to be raped. No information, no preparation – shock and freeze.

Sadistic strategic abuse is planned and is always non-consensual action towards the victim that it takes all the victim's power till the victim is losing all inner empowerment. You only lie there like an observatory aim – just a piece of meat – that they can watch, observe, learn on me again 'FOR FREE' and later on talk "About 'me', without me". It's good, after all, for this teen who I was back then, we were not at the same university or neighbourhood or training/work area later on. But look – they came just like that, took everything that they wanted FOR FREE and went out. The same happened to me and on me last years when I was healing.

There are so-called gurus, mentors or leaders who will take the lead over you and your life without your consent and out of context again and again and again – in the healing world also. If we talk about the therapeutic world, they will even more, intervene with even more sadism. From a place of sadistic strategic abuse, they will come into your life and lead your life through their sadisms (their sadistic lenses). It's very important to CONFRONT them globally and have the courage not only to confront but also to report them. In my place, it was always impossible as they were or too big or had too much power over me as all was planned from behind, or they were simply more than one and here is very needed one more component – that I was always alone in this. Sadistic strategic abuse is connected with denied freedom of sexual energy in perpetrators, which also reaches a cultural/spiritual level. Lack of life energy and pure liveliness in the sadistic communities because of patriarchate culture creates collective tension from their rigid minds. They laugh from any form of child-like beautiful full of aliveness energy that flows in a healthy human. Sadists have no idea about this kind of possibility. Such a level of aliveness forms aggression and hatred inside of sadists, which is based on jealousy what is happening, finally on releasing this sadism on one innocent who is made by all of them their scapegoat.

I had a chance to be a whiteness of this abuse personally when I accidentally was put for 3 days to such place as mentioned before to sadistic psychiatric hospital, and only because there was no place for women to put on so called by someone a 'detox.' So as there was only a detox place for men in this hospital section, they put me in the section with women only – a psychiatric one. Someone proposed to me that it would be a good idea (from their perspective, I needed detox – remember it's always somebodies perspective), and I suppose to wait 7 days and after this go to the treatment centre. That was the time in March 2004 when I decided by myself to stop drinking alcohol, choosing not to be like my father in drinking (I also decided to stop drinking coffee for some time that time, btw). It's more than 18 years ago now. So I accidentally spent 3 days in a place where were only women, but the place was in a section of psychiatry as there was the only place to put me there 'for free' on wait. I was only drinking alcohol and stopped it by myself as a decision from me for myself. I never returned to drinking again, even though I was never an alcoholic ("Can you sign this document otherwise, I cannot offer you the treatment for free"). So being put in the psychiatric section for 3 nights and waiting for transportation to this treatment centre, I have to admit I have never seen such dehumanisation, except in my home place (*I Will Tell, Anyway!* by Ewa Lawresh) on my eyes that an innocent young woman was totally sadistically out of humanity caged there and put into belts while the next nights she was dehumanised fully being half-naked. This could be called 'a treatment without panties' – an innocent still teenager treated sadistically like a caged animal – again – without panties. She was there put under drastic sadistic abuse while she was fighting and fighting like an animal in this trapped situation, stuck on the table, her sexual organs were exposed, she was cached by the workers, who put her on this table and nodded her hands and legs, so she was entrapped

– sadistically caged. This is not humanity and a place of healing – it's sadism! Not healing. And what about the workers of this institution? They could say, let's say, after all, explain their behaviour – "I just work in here," "I just do what am asked for," "They pay me, so I do," releasing all the responsibility onto the institution. Wasn't this like under Holocaust? They all took part, or they used others who took part in sadism – red face (*I Will Tell, Anyway!* by Ewa Lawresh).

Sadistic strategic abuse is not based on consent. There is no consent – boundaries are constantly crossed on any possible level. "May I sadistically abuse you or use you and laugh at from this when you are miserable or bleeding on the floor?" Or, "Are you okay to be sadistically abused by me as your perpetrator, that we both have fun or if you do not, I will do, instead of you?" Consent and non-consent – I was abused without consent all my life. Sadists have no idea that there is something like – consent. Sadistic strategic abuse is based on sadistic agenda, so for them, there is no place for consent. If a rapist wishes to rape, there is no consideration for the rapist about the consent – "May I rape you from behind?" I was not asked ever, "Ewa, are you interested in being abused on your sexuality publicly with us perpetrators, perverts, laughing "clowns" and those who made a profit at the same time from your person also by the way removing you from the market?" I was never ever asked, "Ewa are you willing to be statistically strategy abused by us as communities, we will simply charge on you?" For the sadists would feel at least awkward asking for the consent to abuse me because sadistic strategic abuse is based on actions made from behind.

If there is no consent, that means that the boundaries are not respected. It's simply abuse and usage on innocence. I was never asked if I would wish to protect my boundaries when the attack was from behind, like, "Ewa, we plan to destroy you publicly and your precious face, would you mind protecting yourself with your boundaries when we are doing this?" To input sadistic abuse on the person, the most important part is to weaken the victim out of their consciousness and awareness. That's why there is no place to say "yes" or "no." Remember. The person who is strategically abused from behind doesn't know what is happening. And as long the person doesn't know what is happening is, more and more, going into a place of disorientation in which is no orientation about what is happening. What is bringing even bigger traumatisation. The person who is chosen by sadists out of consent is never asked for permission or consent.

If you abuse a person who disagrees with being abused, it's abuse – more – it's a crime. If the person is not aware of being abused, it's an even bigger crime. So we are not talking about the consent between, let's say, sadists and the victim in receiving sadism, but here we have something called as planned from behind to take advantage of the vulnerable one. Setting boundaries is very hard for the victim because the victim does not know what is happening. I was in this exact place – I always was in the place of not understanding what was happening in social life as everything was always planned behind my back – upfront! And I was never informed about it – obviously. I from myself was taking this as people have good intentions (as I had good intentions and no hidden agenda under, I would even not invent that there is a hidden agenda to plan harm towards the other) projecting my inside for good intentions. As per the hidden agenda, there is a tremendous difference between people who wish you well and people who wish you bad.

Sadistic Extremes

Sadists can go to extremes towards the victim, and through these extremes in the victim, they create waves of charge and discharge. It's almost like there is no limit for the sadists, they will cross all the limits in the victim to reach the hidden agenda of what is a crime, and while committing a crime, they will accuse the innocent one of these crimes. The outcome of extremes for sadists is a gratification to the extent that the sadist is pumped with the energies inside. So it's almost like, let's say, if we blow up the balloon, so the blowing of sadistic energy is going into the balloon, and the balloon is growing and growing in the sadist through the victim's reactivation until it blows out entirely. The sadist will not stop until is fully released with this sadistic energy onto the victim.

So the sadist will not take the balloon and will just blow in, so within, let's say, six times. For them, the balloon needs to blow out after exposition. That means that the victim needs to give their reaction to the fullest, to the end until the victim is burned out or gets a stroke or, let's say, chronic illness. This is a real activity trap for the victim with no way out. So this is something that the victim is in a relation all the way conditioned as a child, as being a problem. So, of course, everyone has different psychological makeup by the programmed blocks and specific conditions based on complexities, so yes, also everyone will experience this sadistic dynamic differently.

And there has to be a special match where the sadists can be interwind together with the victim. So there has to be special sadistic bonding as a condition created in the victim's childhood or even earlier when the innocent is already in their mommy's belly. That means if the pregnant woman is already experiencing sadistic abuse, the child inside of her as well. So the stress response in the mother is creating an unborn child in the same environment outside and inside as the mother is already experiencing this. So the child, when is a grown-up, will look unconsciously for sadistic stress bonding and re-inventing it unconsciously on the same intensity which was created already in mommy's belly. This will be brought to the innocent from any sadistic community – as a "sadist environment" where it can be pumped unconsciously. It's not the fault of the innocent one who is unconsciously stepping around it and not recognising that it's not healthy. If the programming was this, created this way, it will also be repeated for the innocent one this exact way. When we think about this, it's never a choice. That would be surprising that the innocent person would desire by choice to become a victim of thousands of sadists or a smaller number... whatever, as I said many times in this book, it's non-consensual sadism, in most forms as sadistic backstabbing (so zero orientation and zero consent with the innocent one) what is poured towards the victim for the matters to rise on the innocent one by the sadists.

Unfortunately, the unconscious patterns of intensity from childhood will take the lead, but it's never a choice that the victim could think, "And now I will go somewhere to experience sadism..." For the victim, the sadism which is experienced is never something planned. Still, the sadistic perpetrator plans this through various strategies already mentioned above – and mostly when sadists plan to remove the innocent one from the place where the innocent one is not any more USEFUL for the sadists, in any way, anyway. Sadists always wish to look good. Their outside face has to look good – the patriarchate society works only this way. When a person becomes a human with a spectrum of feelings – it's already destroying this person's face and reputation somehow. Then those responsible for destroying someone's reputation can collect together in one place and laugh at the innocent one who is now under psychological tortures – in full traumatisation. So the victim of strategic sadism – as one who already feels some familiarity in the constellation with the observers as sadists (while being under sadism) – both parties and observer and the victim will perceive this all from different perspective/s. It's remarkable that the observers form a sadistic group who are not inputting sadism directly – they only observe – they already are taking part in sadism as well. They are passive sadists. They become sadistic observers who, most of the time, think, "It's good, it's not happening to me," "It's good, it's not for me/about me," "It's good, I did not have to go through this (rather her)" and all will take part in this as for them it's a fun party/comedy show, you name it, the same as for their main perpetrator, who is directly inflicting sadism, they all will join, and they will enjoy. Sometimes sadists choose you for their representation even without informing you about this. For the representation they chose me was that they included me in what was not my representation as a chosen one, and most importantly, there was not me in it. I was like a child in the dust, blind under trauma and reactivated fully in my early childhood experiences.

The caged human in me appears while healing in me as I am going from adventure in my years of meeting many people and experiencing a lot of interesting experiences, which were reaching extremes based on my childhood. I was kidnapped, and sadists earned on me. When I was healing, many sadists made a usage – career on me and earned money on me, they raised on me at my own cost, the same way as sadists did this to me in my childhood. Sadists are even so sadistic that they will put innocent one under psychological tortures to gain some kind of knowledge to earn money later on – on it. It's sadism. A group of men did a business on me when I was kidnapped, and this childhood program did repeat the last years when I was under healing and from men and from women. I was trapped in my family house with my father also and later on trapped with my mother also.

Sadistic Perversion

Sadists will create certain associations connected with their pervasive obsessive envious thinking based on perversion. Sadists are perverts. That's why all the plan is perverted and is around sexual topics and possession of the object. The main motive behind this is to possess the sexual object. From their insecurities, sadists feel jealous, so most times, they isolate the object explaining, "I will take care of you, but I will have to take all the control over your life" or "If you cheat on me, I will destroy your life" – it's a threat and more a case to immediately calling the police. Sadists don't see this. They see that they can say this towards you with huge proudness on their face. They decide about you, not you decide about yourself. And they destroy – yes – they destroy your life whenever they want. It's not the only component of sadistic grandiose narcissism – control and power over – but there is something based on jealousy (sadistic, malicious narcissism), which comes from tremendous smallness of the sadists. When I was healing, I was in many places in the workshops where very different situations were happening simultaneously. So there was a spread of information about me in a strategic sadistic pervert way (sadistic, malicious sociopathy). For example, now I am changing gender (I identify from early childhood with being cisgender, and I have never had any issues personally). Sadists were making faces, their mouths forming sarcastic smiles were sadistically leaking words of abuse. The sadistic show was not about Ewa, but rather about the sadistic perverts who are beholding eyes and ears with sadistic madness, and they are putting me in the middle of it as their (problem) sexual object (earning on this occasion a lot of money on me without my consent – again what is a crime and a case to the Supreme Court). Perverse arousal around and in the sadists was reaching pick. It showed a lot about sexual perversity in sadistic communities and their attitude toward innocent person. They love public rapes – and what all these sadistic communities showed, they also love sociopathic rapes from behind.

The most that saved me in these perverts' sadistic, sexually charged on me societies was that most of the time, I did not know what was happening around my person (I was born with a diverted mind, so I did not take publicity the way an average person takes). However, they knew what was happening around my person as that was planned. Sadistic strategic abuse is based on obsessive perverse, and it's connected with envy and hatred. It's an even bigger place of intensity, which will lead to the destruction of any innocent person as the intensity in the sadistic community is so high (this point is crucial). The only way to safe self is to leave forever such sadistic communities / sadistic family system / sadistic friends who are backstabbing on any possible occasion – and even for this sometimes can be paid small amounts of money between themselves.

Sadistic perversion is not happening on the outside. Sadistic stories as lies inside of the perpetrator are not for real as it's all happening inside of the perpetrator who is in the past, and all is based on the past. Sadists, from the eyes of the perversion of sadistic beholders, see their thoughts as facts, and they act upon these thoughts – it's all in the sadists, and it's all in sadistic communities.

Sadistic perverts have a mental representation of sadistic perversion in the public eye, it is connected with something inside them. What brings sexual arousal is something like sadistic fake "aliveness" – arousal to act and behave a certain way. This is not connected with any true aliveness and healthy energy management. They are under sadism, they almost look like a little bit lighting up, and they are laughing from this place then they are shadowing down for a moment till they again are lighting up towards sadists' laughter at. They are loud, and they are in a perversity place.

So can we call a girl that she's a prostitute just after when she was raped, and she is trying to report this as is looking for help or more, she is pushed to report this not at the police station, but rather to 3 older men who are reminding her the same rapist's experience she just had a few days before. No one sees that others are trying to minimize the experience and even blame her by minimizing the actions done toward her. It's a sadistic tactic of blaming the victim. They can also entirely deny there was a rape. For anyone as an innocent one would be devastating to hear this. Moreover, this would be devastating for the teenage girl I was at that time – it devastated me fully.

My life was entirely destroyed by public and private perverse. The more they laughed at me in a state of deep trauma, the more sadistic perverse they felt. They had a representation in their mind of something that they have had at that time and what was absolutely not relevant to what was happening in NOW. Sadism is a very intense state of perversity, there is no sensuality, delicacy in the perception, presence of now and never in the body as it's out of embodiment. That would be very irritable for the sadist to see the world with delicacy. So this sadistic perverse has to go very far for a long time and then to the moment of the place of release. That's why sadism is not stopped in the beginning by the perpetrator, as they do not let this fade in themselves, as the sadism is done slowly and for a long time to raise the intensity in the sadist, to release this all finally on the innocent one. Healing wounds of sexual abuse is the most important part of dismantling the stories written in childhood, in the innocent one, and all the mental representations based on created in the stories in the other people's minds about the innocent victim. Sadists are in the stories of their own minds but not in victims' stories in the way the perpetrator perceives it. When I was healing, I was dragged from behind to the other people's stories and now more – highly publicly prosecuted for their own stories in their own heads without any reality and factuality! And there were only representations outside as words from their mouths ("About 'me', without me"), out of facts.

Sadist is a capsuled perpetrator who has all their own representation of who they are capsuled inside of them, and all that they talk about is this what they talk about from this sadistic closed capsule out of any reality and factuality. They use the eyes of the sadistic beholder as they have only these eyes and then use sadistic voices to justify actions based on sadistic insecurities towards the innocent person. The more innocent the person, the more this person will be made a scapegoat by the sadistic perverts.

Effect of Sadism – Reactivation

So what we are observing under strategic sadistic abuse the victim is in reactivation. This is happening in many places as a physical field (for example, the hospital/ psychiatric hospital/treatment centre) and also under neuro-psycho-socio-biological tortures. See what was also happening in concentration camps as the sadists were refusing to accept their guilt as is in many stories that there was something like delusional thinking in the sadists and almost an art of self-deception that the perception of the information was different than what the victim truly was experiencing this exact moment. It's crucial as this also happened to me in Australia when a group of people attacked me. The sadist who inputs sadism does not see the innocent person as a human. For them, the human is only a targeted object. The sadists are out of any humanity. A victim is an object treated as a plastic bottle found on the sand, while the sadists can put a stick into this bottle or do whatever they wish to do (so manipulate the bottle and navigate the mentioned stick the way they wish). For the sadists, it's only an object to manipulate. It's not a human and will never be seen as a human by the sadists.

Sadist needs human reactions and the best from the place of reactivation. So the object needs to gurgle, squeeze, cry, or give any other voices like under consensual sadism (what some prefer) – this way, the sadist is rising. So the victim is laughed at frankly for being a human under tortures without consent – mostly, all the observers do not know that being a human under tortures will be at least hysterical. If you have access to feelings (and you are not yet evolved human with processed traumas and all your past), you will go under tortures into reactivation. The voices sadists like are almost like voices close to any animal voices. Sadist operates on body sadistic level "Meow" for example, there has to be a reaction as tone of voice. You have to see this through these lenses – these are sadistic lenses – the eyes of the sadistic beholder. For the sadist does not matter that there is NO consent, mostly for the person with a very high public position. There has to be "blood" – an effect that "screams." There has to be something that the sadist can see the reaction on. If we see a healthy human – access to feelings and feeling in now – this is the most important self-empowerment component. To feel and to be vulnerable at the same time. It's the strength of a healthy human (with a processed past, it's even more sparkly and aligned with health). Sadists want you to "feel under traumatisation" – it's the biggest and the highest false empowerment for the sadists (even the feelings are not theirs). They rise when they see you suffer, and they all are about agenda. In this place in a patriarchate culture, you lose your so-called reputation – it means now you are a feeling human under reactions and under full reactivation (through, for example, psychological tortures, so through traumatisation), but you do not see it as an observer – you only see a person who is under reactivation. What is devastating in the 21st century is that it's "shameful" for the patriarchate culture if you are a human now having access to feelings and more publicly? Oh no! From now on, you will lose a job or friends, or you will be thrown away from the community or even entire society because they are not under "reactivation" (and how come they are not under psychological tortures – because they are focused on how to torture the victim – so they are busy in this place). So sadists don't feel – they cannot. It was the same under Holocaust when the perpetrators, after inflicting tortures, were going on living – coming back to their families and eating dinner, enjoying the warmth of the fireplace while others were dying "on the other side" of the camp...

The sadist is the most deadly in these circumstances where there is no reaction at all when the other suffers at the same time. They will make it a fun whole comedy show, though, and will laugh at it. It's not healthy human behaviour. There is a tremendous difference between a person who is under reactivation under trauma, the person who is a sadist and is in a response place, and the person who is under "reactivation" as is a human in a full spontaneity with healthy processed sexuality, and there is a difference between a person who is healthy and is in a response place. Sadistic commentators – remember – are mostly in a place of disconnection and judgement out of context – as they are in past and negative projections while not feeling anything at all. Sadists are looking for gratification – the only gratification here is – an effect of the sadism – reactivation. Sadist needs intensity for the pumping energy inside. So they use the victim to pump the energy and then release it. They this way have to look for to use the innocent one. How many adults tend to laugh at the child who is in reactivation? How many teens and young people committed suicide under reactivation? Sadist is consciously or unconsciously creating an inner circle of sadist's energy. Sadist is looking for the prolongation of reactivity in the victim – this also in patriarchate culture ruins the reputation of the innocent one – remember. Sadist is creating psychological invasion and input this onto the victim. Sadist is always in the past – so no matter what sadists will tell you about the innocent one – never believe (first, it's a sadist's story based on their inner sadism; second, it's personal for the sadist, so it's a projection – a layer of sadism; third it's a lie as sadists never say the truth as are out of reality from their own intensity and if they will say anything about the victim it's always exaggerated in braces of extremes). Sadist does not perceive themselves as human so has no access to humanity, compassion and a healthy way of processing emotions.

Sadistic Punishment

So the victim will not go away as long as there is such severe harm that there is illness or an attempt of suicide from feeling sadist's tension towards the victim, which is inputted that the person cannot stand this tension anymore.

Sadist is inputting potential harm into the victim as a strategy. There is reactivation in the victim, then the sadist will punish the victim for the reactivation, and when the victim is punished for it, there is in this punishment release in a sadist. That's why sadists love so much inflicting punishment and public prosecution based on persecution. It's all about punishment because it gives for the sadists power over, and they can finally blow out their sadism which they feel inside themselves, onto the victim. Sadistically inside, their own sadistic energy is looking to be released through some kind of ridiculous sadistic show that has nothing to do with reality and humanity, as laughter from somebody's misery is not humanity as it's pure sadism. The bigger show, the bigger excitation, the more excitation, the more sadistic energy is pumped in, and as an aftermath, the bigger the sadistic release is going to happen. Sadists have to repeat this circle all their life. So there has to be a special combination of all of these sadistic components. There must be humiliation and dehumanisation, including complete, slow motion degradation. So that means that there has to be always something that is about power over and control, that the sadist is always over the victim. The smaller the sadist inside, the bigger the sadist outside. The victim does not have to be big, but the victim is always alone. There is no place for treating the victim as a human as the sadist does not possess components of being a human.

One of the strategies of the sadistic strategic abuse is the show about the victim ("About 'me', without me") – under which the victim loses publicly face. The more exposure, the bigger the audience and the bigger release inside the sadists. It's happening as the victim needs, in the eyes of the sadists, to be degraded – then the sadist feels somehow released that the victim finally had to go through this humiliation – and the sadist feels this sadistic energy. It's their non-capability to cooperate with their own energy, they pop up the gratification of being over the victim. When the victim is entrapped, the sadist feels this power over and only from this pick point the sadist can release this sadistic energy onto the outside. And remember, sadists need to do this over and over again. We can see this in many circumstances in life when the group of men or women cannot stand the aliveness of one person – for example, a woman and her sexual energy while she shines around just for being who she is. Sadists cannot stand this. They immediately become jealous. The more formed group with more sadistic participants, the more these sadistic people will attack the innocent targeted object rather than resolve this within themselves and their repressed sexuality. It's definitely the problem of this sadistic group/system/community/society rather than one person – unfortunately, the targeted sexual object. It's so-called group/community sadistic madness starting now, and slowly, sadists are going out. Nowadays, this is a sadistic social justice and public sadistic prosecution based on persecution – a complete madness moreover accepted somehow by the law. The one who is seen and more exposed by the sadists is now under sadistic social justice, and sadistic madness shared in sadistic communities absolutely without victim's consciousness about this (where in criminal way data of the innocent one now is spread even law will not stop them). No one knows what is true and false anymore, as all are in a state of sharing the same sadistic energy (it's sadistic bonding). They will not call it collective dizziness and that it comes from their sadistic, foggy brains. The innocent is threatened and is the biggest problem of this sadistic system. Then the sadistic system has no other problem than the innocent one – the problem with a capital P.

In the patriarchate culture, they will destroy feminine power in a woman first even though she will not do any actual actions she is falsely accused of or do anything. But sadists want to show their face and shine their face in the victim's light and over the victim – it's a created contrast. This contrast creates a layout for the sadists to destroy innocent person life, career and reputation. So the sadist and me – so the sadist will say let say: "I am reliable, you are not" (scapegoat is truly in traumatisation fully reactivated, it's hard to be reliable while being a scapegoat while scapegoat at the same time is at least 'hysterical' on crying call from early childhood reactivated wounds, or simply fights inside to be alive). So the sadists will continue to say: "You are not reliable," while at the same time, the victim is traumatised by the sadists. They want to be prepared so that nobody will find out who the sadist truly is by turning attention to the "troubled," "rebel" victim as the main "Problem" who is fully traumatised from sadistic psychological tortures about what no one knows. Only what is seen even in the social arena is that the victim proves the negativity spoken about themselves as being under tortures (conscious/unconscious inner ugliness of sadistic beholder)...

How is it seen? By comments on social media, for example. Was there any investigation (proper, legal, formal, supported by law) that anything about the victim has been ever true? No. So how come they all know that what they say is true and about the victim and not about the sadist? Truth is one – sadists see in the scapegoat (made by the sadist) who the sadists are – remember, the voice given to sadists by sadists is a voice of sadism.

Sadist is not interested in showing you publicly in positivity as sadist has no idea what is positivity until sadist has a profit from their "positive" community members – it's melting in sadism now.

Chapter 5

Sadistic Excitement

Innocent people are suffering and being under humiliation, and dehumanisation sadists can even show in a funny way what is one of the biggest expressions of their own release onto the innocent one. The funnier way it is shown, the more sadistic amplitude rises in a perpetrator inside. It can happen in a hidden room of a dark house and in a public arena through amusement and sadistic entertainment like in an animal circus or this way social zoo, for example. Sadist is inventing the strategy, putting the innocent under this strategy and later on punishing the innocent one who is, in fact, "hysterical" and, yes, under interrogation and even surveillance – for this and their reactions. Innocent one is punished because there is blood from the cut wound... punished for the natural way system heals... prosecuted for choosing herself for her own children happiness even! If she cannot be with them right now... prosecuted for being a human... prosecuted for the existence... and the inner fight not to commit suicide and still be alive... even the blood is bleeding... When the victim is being punished for the reaction, what happened to me all my life, personally and professionally also! the consequences for the victim are seen and will be seen if not for some time, so then years or even for a lifetime. And what happens next? In the same way, the innocent victim of the rape is later on punished – prosecuted! for the consequences of the consequences done to the victim! Now the victim is made the ugly one. Sadists have very strong attitude toward making innocence ugly. It's based on the sadists' inside – what is inside – this is what they create outside (remember this, and they speak about themselves, not the other) – but what they create on the outside – they do not create about themselves – they create it all – paradoxically about the innocent one and this is then what is seen publicly. Sadistic strategic abuse is based on punishment. It's about taking everything from the victim, the victim's life, the victim's voice, publicly it looks like – the victim is now shown in negativity (WARNING: no one knows it's the sadists' negativity) while sadists are using the victim's knowledge to show how smart the sadists are (while it's victim's knowledge, inventions, beauty, pureness and genius). Would you believe something like this is possible?

Next, the sadists will inflict pain with amusement. It's almost unbelievable that such things are happening. So we can see this if we take an apple and if we throw it and let's say before we see an apple and it gives a beautiful scent. We can even take a bite of the apple while if we throw this apple onto the wall and again, and again, then we boil the apple, the same apple from the beginning will not look like before. No. Now, suppose we put the pictures of the apple before and the apple after. In that case, we will see how strategic sadistic abuse looks exactly and what inflicted sadistic harm does to an innocent human.

So the outside is devastated. The apple does not serve anymore as the main reason. It can serve any other reason, so if somebody smashes this apple onto the wall, can take control at a distance of two meters and play how far that can go. Sadistic strategic abuse is a long process of destruction in slow motion. Under strategic sadistic abuse, the sadist is operating on a huge level of jealousy and punishment for the reason that the victim is a supply (for example, a knowledge supply for free) on any possible level. Sadist launches their life on the victim, becoming the decision person now over the victim. Sadistic communities, as well as sadistic family systems (both – they NEVER protect innocence), will soak in from the victim and build entire lives and careers on the victim while stopping the victim from growth and independence by imputing cohesive control and power over including complete possible control (also on money level). Sadist is interested in taking everything from the victim to the last "drop of the blood" like a vampire.

There is no consent under strategic sadistic abuse but rather excitement and sadistic dehumanised comedy. Observe how many people laughed at me while I was healing all these years. Observe their faces – are their faces red from sadism? Sadists love doing things with faces (*I Will Tell, Anyway!* by Ewa Lawresh).While I was healing the last years, I experienced only dehumanisation, only humiliation, only degradation, only sadistic prosecution, and lash back with persecution from cults, societies, institutions, organisations and communities. All was happening indirectly by foolishly ridiculing me or directly by closing the doors in front of my face while sadists had the amusement on their own faces again. Frankly, the more is out of context, the more the amusement the sadists have. They express it through laughter and fun while all of the participants as observers (and all in the collective who are the observers) act under sadistic symbolic 'sexual rape' based on the effect – sexual relief under. If you see this this way, what was also done to our mother Earth is seen. Nothing is seen, though, for the whole collective as long as the entire collective is taking part in this 'sexual collective rape'. Sadists are not always blind to the fact that dehumanised object is a human. They act from the place of the power over while observing, inputting sadistic triggers and then, in my case, recording my reactions repeatedly, everything without my consent and everything out of CONTEXT. Reactions are triggered – this way, a traumatic human is built, and it's the nature of it. It's important to understand that rapes are also without consent. It's rape culture and rape communities where all participants take part in the way that if others rape, they also can (innocence is NEVER protected, innocent one though is always USED). And why not, sadists will ask? The responsibility immediately is spread everywhere but not to the participants themselves. And as the responsibility is spread, no one takes it, all touch the innocent one then – their victim, their scapegoat – to the point that the innocent one has this achieved red face (*I Will Tell, Anyway!* by Ewa Lawresh). Then they laugh. While I was healing, I remember when I was in a few meetings with people were, let's say several people were constantly putting on me that I am a man who is interested in a sexual way toward women. Remember, I was still healing incest trauma, and I was in a small, shamed girl place.

The sadistic game was not that I am a woman who is interested in a sexual way towards women, but the sadistic game itself inflicted also changing my gender behind my back without my knowledge about it and later on directly in a sadistic way and laughing at me this way. I have never identified inside of me with any other gender, rather cisgender, while sadists will take advantage of any WORD/single sentence (out of context) the innocent one says. Sadists do this to sadistically mock and bully the victim. So sadistic strategic abuse involves mind sadistic games that put the innocent in survival and traumatisation.

Sadistic strategic abuse is based on false accusations put onto the innocent one while mostly it looks like a show "about the innocent one – without the innocent one." Sadists will for a long time put victim under self-delusion that the victim will not recognise the losses is experiencing at the exact moment. It's happening because the victim can be like, in my case, desperately trying to find safety. Sadistic strategic abuse is about amusement if the observer sees that the innocent person is under sadism and is being laughed at. In that case, they all observe with sadistic interest and sadism themselves, joining the others in this sadism's group together. So more and more observers come and join and take part and say, "Look, this person is threatening this one, come and watch, what a show." They don't help the victim, never, they join the sadistic party. Victim for them stops being a human – is a targeted object now, not a human – from now on, it's the object of sadistic release.

The next entrapment is that the sadistic parent who is feeling this excitement and fascination in this empowerment while at the same time disempowering the innocent one, the sadist, is starting the sadist's game again. So when there is a crying reaction in the victim, this opens full access to emotions in the victim. Again, sadists charge on this and falsely rise. In a sadistic game, there is always a motive (in the end, to reach punishment and, in most cases, if it's public – a prosecution – the biggest peek point dreamed for sadists). The innocent one is weakened and now is in reactivation with no support. So the sadist to gain more power over is telling "If you do not stop crying, I will beat you," so in this case "If you do not stop..., I will..." put whatever they exactly said to you. So now the innocent one reaction has to be stopped, and from this moment, the sadistic oppression and coercive control starts. Everything is made by purpose, and sometimes, in some cases, the more the sadistic show is shown, the more false victory the sadist gains. So the strategy is to make the victim weaker and weaker. So from this place, the sadists are overpowered by fake abusive leverage through the power over the vulnerable one. Please remember one thing – the sadist's game is never ever equal. It's not a fight between two equal people. It's not even a fight between adult and adult while it's important to understand that the person under psychological tortures no matter age is vulnerable (this way is a state of the child's reactivation) and has no protection, as the inside of this person is so vulnerable and so open towards the world that anyone can now harm the innocence. ANYONE. And in this place, the sadist is saying, "If you don't stop crying…" Threats (life-death), intimidation, belittling, humiliation and degradation – all evoked by any kind of tortures and psychological tortures, which again are mostly never seen – when are inflicted and at the moment of infliction from the observer's perspective. In this place – who is the observer/commentator/the chatterbox/judger? Now, what if the observer is the whole community and has never observed the infliction of tortures at the moment of infliction? More… what if the observer is the whole collective?

Remember: sadism is inhuman and has nothing to do with humanity. The perpetrator was informed am pregnant, so more overused the opportunity to put me under traumatisation. Sadists, while informed that the victim is under traumatisation, will take any opportunity to revenge as the victim is in a weaker place already. In sadist, there is no capacity for love, genuine help or compassion. The sadist, while knowing the person is under trauma, will put this person under even bigger trauma to revenge and will observe the desired reaction (so much judged by the observers and commentators without the moment of "infliction") as for the sadist victim's reactivation is a perceived show where sadistic energy is pumped up through the innocence's pain. The sadist now is in amusement and what is after, is the desired release in the sadist itself and, later on, the desired "profit," whatever the agenda is under.

Let's see this through the lens of the slaughterhouse. It is a place where the animal is dying through a special strategic procedure and then is cut slowly step by step with the next strategic procedure, piece after piece. Sometimes tools are exchanged to achieve the next possible piece in the sadist's hands. It's a very strategic way of cutting off all the pieces till the place where from happy running animal we see only left cut meat pieces of this animal – any animal in a slaughterhouse is stopping being an animal and becoming a piece of meat, perceived money, or any other "agenda" as profit. Pieces of meat are selected and sorted in separate places. This was sadism for the killed animal and objectification of the target. This was also done with my life in the last years when I was healing. As previously mentioned, sadists need a reaction from their victim. What sadistic communities will do, though they will judge and punish the reactivated victim rather than the sadists themselves. How come we as humans came to the place of such unfair treatment of the innocent one? Sadist does not feel the innocence and is not innocent. That is why the target has to be innocent. Communities are scared of the final judgment as a believed crucifixion to step into paradise will do crucifixion towards the innocent object. So the fear of one sadist is spreading towards all the group, and it is now collective fear of crucifixion – now there has to be at least someone on the front line or any other scapegoat who can be wrong-done for the whole collective community – as the fear is now released "through" the victim. Fear of public crucifixion of the whole community, conscious or unconscious – fear – the community will do this for their one participant – the chosen "problem" – the one who will pay for this as I paid for the sadistic collective and their sadism inflicted on me. Isn't a paradox? In our society is very clear to observe that the reactivated person is judged rather than the one who is accusing the victim. Sadistic entrapment is based on inputting on the child or innocent one directly as long as there is the archived reaction as a certain mimics or behaviour. This way, sadists are looking for proof of any false accusation they create. Teasing – is not about teasing but about lowering the self-confidence of the innocent one that the sadists can feel power over and possessiveness towards the innocent one. Let's say the parent is teasing the child, while the child is vulnerable and takes everything as heard and all that is exactly said. Children till certain age are like that. They take everything literally and directly as they hear it. In such a child, there is no manipulation based on illusion, any past or future, as the child is now. They don't even know that there is tomorrow and yesterday. What if somebody says – there is a fire – so the child understands that there is a fire, more the child understands that the fire is something that is said about the fire. 'Said' means what said the authority figure or somebody the child trusts. Let's say somebody will say to the child that the potato is an animal. The child understands that the potato is the animal and will keep it in mind. Until this child raises to a certain age of reaching the possible level of imagination and visualisation in their development and later understands what ambiguity is, the child will believe in what is 'said'. Not all children are like this. So the same child can also one day find out from the other person that the potato is a vegetable and not an animal, and the figure was only... teasing? the child... So the person in this age or a certain stage of development is taking everything that it is from the perspective of the child's mind's development.

Sadistic strategic abuse is very often done this way with victims by 'teasing' them on purpose and then laughing at the innocent one in front of the audience, making an innocent one stupid – in fact, to lower the value of the innocent one in front of the others that the innocent one has no place to take their own life back (it's a strategy to make the innocent one less worthy). In this place, sadists will show the innocent one as psychiatrically ill to control this person's life for the matter "Well you see, she is not controlling her life, I have to" will say sadists (while controlling her accounts, bank accounts, earnings, access to travelling, access to society – here will spread lies that the person has no access to the society as already society believes the sadist, not the innocent one who can be already half damaged psychologically by the sadists behind the scene). Unfortunately for the person at a certain age, teasing does not work, and it turns into being bullied and experiencing sadism. For me and teasing and bullying is a form of sadism. If we take a person under trauma – the person goes into bigger reactivation and then threat and intimidation, finishing in a place of traumatisation and victimisation at the end. The sadists will call it "It was just teasing," "Don't you know I was joking?", etc. Remember – sadists NEVER joke, it's not a sense of humour – it's cruelty based on hidden AGENDA.

As an example of sadistic strategic abuse between a parent and the child is the sadistic game "I don't like you. I don't love you." It's a game to get certain reactions from the child and what was also my own experience in childhood. The more reactivation, the higher amusement is in the sadists that the sadists can release themselves on the innocent one while the child is under psychological tortures, it's not a show for the child or an innocent person. Sadist is hanging the innocent person as long as they have a profit on it – they charge themselves and their false importance and grandiose. The child is in the sadistic circus, and after the reactivation appears, the sadist can release themselves and rise falsely on the other. In many cases, such a scene ends with somebodies death, in almost all cases, the dead one is the innocent one. The sadist can hang the person over for a long time with no direct answer keeping silent, and under this silence, they build their false importance. It's a strategy. Rather than giving back a relational answer as reciprocity between the two – the sadist is pumping their own power over with hidden agenda. Sadists have no idea what reciprocity is and what loving kindness is. The sadistic game towards the innocent one, "I don't like you. I don't love you," said in a repetition – sadists can even say in a repetition directly even with conviction saying it and looking deeply in the child's eyes. So the child first doesn't understand it the way that does not believe it, doesn't think that it's true. In prolongation, it creates suffering in a child. The innocent is looking for the love from the caregiver. The child wants to be loved. In the same way, the innocent is looking for love from the beloved one as the innocent one wants to be loved. The innocent one can say, "No, it's not true. You love me." The game continues in repetition, which creates sadism and sadistic game. But for the child, it's real. It's not a game. The innocent will take it as it is – just as it is. What sadist does is a sadistic game based on power over and control over the victim's emotional state until the victim is in their trap. It's sadism as there is an intention of the amusement on the other person's pain and suffering. The main motive is that the child is suffering through the emotional reaction – the sadists have now power over the victim, and the victim is under full control. So the child starts crying because feels not loved. Can start screaming, "No! You love me! Love me! Say that you love me!" Now, the child's conditioning of the sadistic abuse is created as the child takes it personally. Some can see the suffering and come and say – "I was only joking," again by diminishing what truly happened, not feeling the victim's pain, and not taking responsibility for this. It's a form of sadistic tortures – it's sadistic usage of the innocent. Think... for what such game is even created on the relational level? To see this deeper, the child will be in a relational field conditioned for something going into intensity in the child's nervous system. It is distress which created after all reactivity, and this reactivity is now inside the child, conditioned forever. This is what the sadists wanted – a reaction in a full reactivation state – it's what the sadists have been looking for from the early beginning. Now finally, the sadists can take control over and punish the innocent one for reactivation – for the blood pouring from the wound. This is the only enjoyment and excitement for the sadists from sadistic manipulation or attack, etc. This will create a reaction the sadist wants to perceive and wants to receive. And now the sadistic show is starting.

Chapter 6

Sadistic Public Smear Campaign

anging the innocent under prosecution is the next sadistic tactic and a way of living to gain profit. The innocent is hanged on waiting for offered affection from the sadist, and the innocent is affected and as was shown before, while the sadist is withdrawing without any real information why till the innocent sweat and burn out. It's a strategy. The main aim here is to evoke in a victim their reactivity – when it appears in an innocent – an innocent can be seen from the outside as a "hysterical" (CIA experimentations on innocent victims without trial – it's a trial itself) person so long that the person is traumatised and thrown onto turmoil trough tortures in any-way. Sadist plans this as it is based on their own power over. The more the victim begs, the more the sadist feels domination and sexual empowerment through hatred towards the victim (there is agenda under). The victim is only a target for the sadist to raise their own power over and charge and recharge sadistically inside. They love to charge on the innocence as the vulnerable child/teen/adult is already entrapped in the sadistic sexual game based on power over – collective healing through me – without me in it ("About 'me', without me"). Sadistic laughter everywhere – sadistic cackling based on their own crimes – never ever equal sadists and their victim – never ever equal starting point, middle point and end point. When the victim is in a vulnerable place attacked by the sadists, they can, for example, as a sadistic abuse, record the victim in the most vulnerable situations, this is planned, so this means sadists know what is going on, but the victim does not know it. So let's imagine a person in reactivation and now is stuck, is under such threat that the person can neither fight nor flight, can do nothing and has to swallow it all to remain silent as the sadistic perpetrator records everything from now on. The victim has to swallow all the "bleeding" inside. Silence... What happened to me publicly while I was under traumatisation like a collective demo on my own cost and the most drastic on my own kids' cost for this sadistic show recorded and publicly shown (my kids were bullied also being under the age of 10 for no reason – for the lies of my perpetrators – who will pay for this now?). I, without my awareness, was stimulated from behind (all was hidden from the observers), under psychological tortures, and manipulated so that the observer did not see the manipulations – the only that the observer saw about me – was the reactivation and actions based on reactivation – the observer / the commentator / the judger – saw the object out of context – what also means defamations and slander started immediately.

All this is image/voice exploitation, which again touches on the objectification of the target and data abuse of the innocent one. In these images, the effect of the shot can be manipulated for the matter of the exact effects of the hidden agenda of the sadists.

Sadists show only the effects of the tortures – sadists do not show the tortures themselves. It's a sadistic strategy. The strategy is to put the innocent one from a shocking place to the place of continuity of psychological tortures while the innocent one is left entirely alone. So it was a total entrapment while the victim is losing complete orientation of what has happened. Now come into action the group of the observers who charge themselves on the victim, on the victim's life, on the victim's knowledge/ideas and the victim's kids' life. Now start gossip, defamation and slander (remember, in most countries worldwide, it's a crime – in this case, crimes made by all communities). The more false accusations, the more slander and defamations are shown (and the more crimes are made). Anyone sees the context – everyone sees the effects. Sadists in this place find the full opportunity to act from the power over. The victim is stuck in reactivity. When the child goes through psychological tortures and is entrapped by the sadists, the child is totally conditioned to the survival mode on the other. Now the wound is opened and is fully "bleeding," with all the effects as an aftermath of what happened to the victim.

Remember, sadists have agenda, they have no idea how to be – they only do, and if they do, they do sadism. An innocent person does not have agenda. This difference is creating an abyss. In my place was that I was an incest victim, sadists were imputing even more wounds as per lies about me – for them, I am under healing sexually exploited 'boy' accused of harassment (no, there was no harassment in Australia). What an abyss. Can you see through the eyes of the sadistic beholder? Incest wounds are not to heal – a sexually exploited 'boy' accused of harassment does not exist here – who exists is a wounded girl trying to be alive and heal the incest wounding. Yes, there was only sadism on the line towards the incest, nothing more than this.

It's significant to see the situation and what happened. Let's say we are observers of the situation where the woman is raped. And the effect is that she is now unstable – oh yes, she is crying – oh yes, she is trying to explain something to the sadistic perpetrators who just charged on her sexually. And let's say somebody is recording such a situation from the outside, out of context. So we can have two extremes of the referee, as first – the perspective of the observer, and second – the perspective of the targeted object. This is a psychological entrapment that involves observers in their own judgment about the person's character undermining all the character of the raped one – oh yes, she is in reactivation – but who does not feel? The one who is in the reactivation or the one who is inflicting sadism? She feels, but it's overwhelming. Sadists don't feel – they charge sexually until they release sadism. Sadist is not interested in the victim now – they experience false relief as could charge on the victim. Remember, reactivation of the innocent one under trauma is not what exactly happens to the person as it can be something more complex you cannot even imagine, it also is not who the person is as it's only traumatic reactivation – if we speak about the exact example. The innocent one under rape is not a stable accountant you meet every day. The innocent one under a life/death attack is not a stable, reliable businessman you have known for years. Even looking for the child, the innocent one under trauma is no longer a stable, happy smiling pal from your work. They all suffer they all are under addiction, they all, if no one will ever know what did happen, will be recorded, and all 3 videos under their reactivation will be set on the media show now, and their life will be ruined as sadists felt jealousy that mentioned as examples accountant, businessman and pal from your work let say, healing person – they all are in open trauma now. Strategic sadistic abuse is based on the above.

While I was under trauma, my all character and personality were entirely undermined by who I am as a human. There were created such stories that sadistic gossipers started even believing in it themselves (remember about the game Chinese whispers). Gossips from first hand – changed through working on the early beginning from hidden agenda, jealousy and hatred – are any more any first-hand information but instead only based hatred sadistic sentences from "About 'me', without me" (and paradoxically only about the sadist).

The innocent one is under planned sadistic attack by a group of sadists, and what the observer sees from the outside – is a totally different point of view. The observers do not see the picture entirely, and the picture fully is what the person – is experiencing through tortures, and it's based on what is done to this person also. So the perception of anyone involved is totally different. The observer sees what is inside their own eyes from the outside, but it's not feeling what the targeted person under tortures is feeling. It's very important to remember that the targeted object is under reactivation inside, and its nervous system is attacked directly. Why? The sadists are not experiencing weakening, but they are experiencing power over from planned attack. It's like a balance between two people energetically – the victim is getting smaller, and the sadist/s as a group is rising in a way that they are empowered in sadistic abuse. Why? The sadists know the plan, as they plan this, so they know... The victim does not know.

From the observer's perspective, when the observer is observing that the person was raped, the observer can see a person who is not stable, whose face is red (*I Will Tell, Anyway!* by Ewa Lawresh) and full of expressions or is simply in shock, then starts crying, and is trying to explain what happens to them. Everything is disturbed in this person, entrapped in shock, the spelling is not clear, the writing is not clear, and even the message can seem to be unclear what they want to say. When the observer is observing, it's almost like it can be full of assumptions. Of course, what is always happening is false accusations about the object's personality as no one knows what is happening with/inside the victim. The person is in the full process of experiencing it, while the observer is in the process of false assumptions and false accusations about the victim's personality and, in general, who the victim is.

It's not any more about the object's behaviour, but now

the whole person is judged, and their whole personality is undermined to zero. The person is not the person experiencing something anymore, but the person is, for example, a projected 'sick monster' for others or just a project. While these are sadists who are expressing aggressiveness toward the targeted person by waiting till this person is in reactivation. The context here counts a lot as the observer does not see the context! The targeted object is in the experience, is absolutely inside of it as a living organism. So the targeted object – as the observed person who is experiencing reactivity inside is in a situation, and this person can be aware or not aware of what is really happening to them even to express it in words, in the emotional reactivity, the person is in survival response. For the person under observation can be the place of the feeling of being under attack. The targeted object is losing control, as is in trauma response. Their nervous system is destabilized more and more because it is additionally harassed and stalked on a daily basis. Can you imagine? Here is the question: Who should go to a psychiatric hospital – the one under reactivation so the person under traumatization, or the person who is hanging the innocent one under prosecution, inflicting full sadism?

Indeed, the person under trauma needs normal human support, understanding, compassion, loving kindness and a safe place to recover. At the same time, whole sadism should be reported and investigated on the perpetrator's side. Only the sadistic perpetrator, sadistic family system, sadistic social justice, and sadistic communities all have to pay a harsh price for sadism on innocence. It's a very crucial difference between who should be investigated and who should be under interrogation… surveillance and control. Unfortunately, our unhealthy society is preoccupied with being focused on the victim and their reactivity under psychological tortures rather than the owner of the prosecution of the victim – the sadistic perpetrator/s and sadistic perpetrating communities. The victim is simply suffering from their tortures and, moreover – is a victim in a victim place. It's not the place to judge the one who suffers, it's a place for understanding, love, loving kindness and compassion.

So, even if we go to the example of, let's say, a minor car accident, so the person who was a driver, let's say, was experiencing something like an overreaction, the red face from shock, waving hands, loss of control and remember this human is in pain and suffering. People in survival are generally in a negative mind state. So the observer who is in survival will be very preoccupied with negativity and go onto negative judgement of the personality of the targeted object. While the observer or observers as a formed group, they all have no idea what happened – they are out of the real context. Sadistic observer jumps immediately into the sadistic story – remember this forever – the story with hidden agenda under as an opportunity to, in a fake way, shine or charge their life even on this victim. The targeted object of the sadists is under tortures. Observers are not in it. They observe. So the target and the observers will see and feel (if they have the capacity to feel – this one is crucial the entire situation differently. While I was under collective sadistic strategic abuse from sadistic rape's cultures worldwide, all tried to take part in this calling it – I don't know why? – collective mutual healing. Unfortunately, the one object which is in it and is inside of it – ME – is abused, used and absolutely exploited sadistically the most. Sadists will always find an opportunity to use, abuse and exploit – and they will find it even if there is no opportunity (they will create one underlies). Sadists do not exist if they do not use as usage and exploitation for free of innocent one is their main aim. This was my entire experience while I was healing. This abuse was doing even simple stalkers and additionally stalking perverts. And each one will tell their own sadistic perverse story differently. These people know what is going on, they record, and they know it. The recorded object by perverts does not even know that it is recorded, more in my case, I was in shock and in half mutism back then. They can see things so differently while dependently from the referee – a charismatic showman, chatterbox, sadist on sexual charge-discharge, shy person or dissociated person. Even the stories they refer to have happened at the same time while on a different timeline – as the survival person is in the story rater in reality. Can you imagine? If the storytellers are sadists, they will strategically take photos or videos to show from maliciousness and intensity in themselves, all that can be seen through the sadistic eye of the sadistic beholder. The observer can see the cause of something as a moving object and judge it negatively about the person without keeping this person in positive rather than negative regards. What about the sadists? The sadists are keeping the object in sadistic regards! So from this place, what you hear and see publicly is a public sadistic smear campaign.

So while this sadistic dance is happening, the one who is the targeted object is seeing the effects of sadistic abuse as a reactivation inside of themselves. Feeling it is a result of being in a sadistic situation with the sadist. If we go through this example with the child who is crying now and is somehow blocked not to cry and cannot cry because will be punished, will be beaten, the sadistic pervert will feel amused when the child is crying but does not feel the pain of the child at all as sadist do not feel compassion. They are not capable of feeling compassion as if they would feel it, they would immediately stop the sadistic abuse/use and exploitation for free. They don't feel they are in sadistic excitation about reactivated sadism inside of them.

More, the sadist doesn't want to feel guilty about what did to the vulnerable person. A sadistic pervert has no morals and no ethics when inflicting pain onto the innocent. Sadism is deeply connected with laughing at from the other person's misfortune, called as Schadenfreude. And it's very important to see this because this is something that is undervalued in our sadistic societies and sadistic communities. So it's clear there is an abyss between the sadistic observer and the vulnerable person who is in this situation as an actor, as the person who is feeling and seeing it all from the midpoint of the inflicted sadism. The victim feels the result of the situation as inflicted psychological torturers, pain and suffering. The sadistic observers see only the reactivated person, so if, for example, the person under psychological tortures will fall down, sadists will judge the person as, let's say, "An idiot fall down." Any person on the planet which is under sadistic strategic abuse in prolongation in the form of psychological/physical tortures – every single human will experience inside of them this sadism if the person feels. It's crucial – the targeted object will experience something different, and the observer, as a sadist, will experience something different. Remember what means the two stories will never ever be the same, moreover, the sadist has an agenda, so their story will be absolutely different from reality, an innocent person does not.

Sadists rise (it's a form of being parasites) on public prosecution of innocent (remember contrast). So they will victimise the innocent for a better show. Sadists are not capable of introspection as being an observer of their own feelings while being turned on triggers, they make a projection on a scapegoat surface (her face, her voice, her body, her name, her life – as per her identification as a targeted object) what they are doing. They are cut off from any ethics and morals that they are treating the other human as someone who's not a human – at all.

Strategic sadistic abuse is based on using toxic shame and any possible past information from the victim's past even if this is absolutely made up – and it was in the past – under smear campaign will join the party, more and more sadists who are telling more and more lies for revenge, shining in the other person light, like parasites. Under the sadistic smear campaign, the components of the past are never true as long they are not based on any agenda. If there is any agenda – there is never any truth – as everything told is under the agenda. Now, it all depends on the agenda. In my case, "About 'me'" any sentence behind the back of the innocent one is "without me" in it. And this one is the most used tactics by the sadists. Let's say a front-line person is a fully visible target for all sadists (no never protected even all charge on her, her knowledge and her ideas all the time), more for all narcissists, psychopaths, sociopaths as the target is fully seen and available (who cares now about her safety when she is spread for free). Sadist is using and exploiting – sadists have no idea about any other way of the relationship between the other how to relate – rather only to use. So sadists will use the innocent one for any possible purpose to achieve what they want from always hidden agenda – at least hidden towards the innocent one.

Sadists are stepping from superiority based on their inner smallness, so they don't want the other to shine. From their perspective, the vulnerable person, including small children, is not a human – it's only a targeted object. As an example, there will be the teacher who feels smaller than the pupil while the sadistic teacher feels threatened by the pupil's genius, brilliance and smartness. Such teacher will use their position and their connections to destroy the innocent pupil because she, as a pupil, is shining more than the teacher (with her genius, knowledge and ideas). That means they will try to make fun of the pupil to dimmish the pupil in front of the rest of the class. "You will get a lower mark that you don't think that you are so smart" I heard the teacher's words when I was a child, even though that was child abuse, it was done to me in primary school. Sadists, with their power over, will do this and justify this all by their own position in school or teaching area or any other area like 'healing' or academia. And then also to lower my marks or certification, they put that I don't behave the way they want, even though there was no case. So to attack, as they cannot attack the genius itself for sure, they will attack the child's behaviour. Can you see this? How? They will revoke traumatisation in a child through toxic shaming and entire class persecution.

So the sadists from the place of the patriarchate would also try to silence the innocent to make them smaller, more stupid, and less attractive publicly that they will do everything and criticise this way that the innocent one will go into distraction and submission. People who are paid to destroy the other person's life are sometimes isolated and not see this and not feel morally involved in a crime because sadists are only interested in criminal actions. So, sadistic strategic abuse is about destroying the image of the person by lowering their self-esteem and defeating them in any possible way, in prolongation through a long time, in repetition, by showing only negativity, darkness, and failures of this person in the class area, work area, publicly. And all is about this fake reputation sadists want to create as a contrast.

I have never shined till now in my life because of the

experienced sadistic strategic abuse on me on an ongoing basis my entire life. What sadists do they see that the innocent person rises to the level that scares sadists – in my case in my life, there were many levels of rising to the level of extraordinary: running, mathematics, writing, relationship, business, therapy/neuro-psycho-biology level, and more. Each time I reached the top that I could be much more bigger than ever before, I was always destroyed by the sadists. I have never reached the highest levels on anything till today because of the actions of the sadists. They build careers on me, my knowledge, my effort, my visions and my 'face', but not me – taking it as their own – denying my ownership and authorship publicly in this, including all my healing/inventions last decade or longer.

This is the sadistic tactic – taking all from their victim and later removing the victim from society for profit purposes or throwing the victim away to keep the victim's credit (intellectual property, inventions, ideas) under their own name. It's sadism. Remember – sadism is painful and is an element of grandiose/malicious narcissism mixed with sociopathy and psychopathy. All see it's my name, all see these are my ideas, all see it. But sadists isolate... sadists put their name on this... for points, for profit, for false credited work, for false authorship. It's sadism, as sadism inflicts pain, the pain of losing credit for the work done, the pain for losing profit to feed their own family – this all sadists take for themselves. It's also a crime, as remember – sadism is a crime.

Parasites

Sadism is a parasite action in a prolongation on innocence while producing on innocence slavery. It's a form of dehumanisation of the innocent one by weakening this person through forms of, for example, having access to their accounts/controlling them and telling the innocent one that they do not know what happened with such a serious expression on their face and so highly surprised. It's step by step taking control over the life of the victim.

So all these politics of power it's happening from the beginning of the victim's life in a sadistic family system, in a sadistic school system, within the relation between a sadistic teacher and the student, and then a sadistic work area full of sadistic culture and their sadistic parasite participants. So they don't know what healthy relationships are. They only arise on the other person treating this person as a supply, using and taking the victim's own resources for themselves, they can rise on the victim's name, they can rise on the victim's illness, they can rise on the victim's pain and suffering.

Sadism is based on a sadistic parasite rising. So they will take everything, the knowledge, the position, the materialistic life and will not let the person come back to the city/on the market/ having even ordinary life, and they will isolate the person that will not come back mostly with crucial information – crucial information about the inflicted strategic sadism. They have no capacity to love as they are not in safety as love belongs only to safety. Sadists are constantly on fight 'eating' and abusing and again 'eating' and abusing and using the victim. So degradation of the inner sense, the exclusion, disassociation, and destroying them, inputting less and less, while showing in sadistic societies that the vulnerable one is "less than" and cannot simply have human rights because is the problem for them...

It's very important to understand that sadists are parasites, and they are using other people for their own aims while they are most empowered using positions and titles. And they are the most hidden one of who they indeed are. So sadists act always against what is human and humanity, and once they start their actions against innocent, they do not stop till the end. This means they from the early beginning dehumanise the object of their cruelty. This is crucial because these are sadists who are the most scared of dehumanisation, facing shame and degradation, and being public stupidity or being called idiots. And this comes from patriarchate – belittling in my case – Ewa, a woman – to the place of making her a stupid sexual object and then treating her like a "stupid little whore." So they don't see a girl/woman in a "stupid little whore" – they just defined their sexual object – no, there is no a girl anymore, and there is no a woman anymore – there is only a prostitute from now on. And then, as per – being made – they treat her as a prostitute. Even though she's not a prostitute so, to stay still as sadists, they will find a justification for their own sadistic eyes of sadistic beholders. And they will believe in this, they will minimise the sadistic abuse (we use her image? She builds our companies? Oh no, she will never get credit for the impact she has done, and as well she will never be paid for this). Paradox – she is paying for their inner sadistic toxins, but she is not paid for her work or more she is not paid for – the usage on her – what they made on her for their own personal/professional aims. It's a crime – every action of sadists is a crime and is against human rights and is against the law, and it's always a case to the Supreme Court.

Media will involve as a parasite to pump up even more as the innocent scapegoat brings them by usage on her – topics and scandal – if there is no scandal, there will be a scandal created by the lies and false accusations created by sadists. Sadists use scandals to evoke certain emotions in people and then to gain a strategically planned aim.

Repayment – I Don't Want YOUR Sorry

Once I was attacked by a group of people, and when they attacked me from many directions, a few of them at once, the attack was towards my body until I was harmed and bleeding in two places. They were harassing me, dehumanising and one of them slapped my buttock from behind. One of them ran out towards me screaming, "Didn't he say sorry, didn't he say sorry?" in a place of explanation of one of the perpetrators' behaviour. I looked at them all and said, "I don't want his sorry." Do you get this? The perpetrators' sorry never work. They need to REPAY fully for their actioned harm – this is the only resolution – they have to REPAY for the crimes.

Chapter 7

Sadistic Persecution

So now comes punishment based on prosecution, leading to persecution (aka 'ill-treatment' including in it ill-society and many treatment communities paradoxically). So the 'crying reaction' is now a kind of 'blood' from the wound created by the sadist. What arises from it in the victim is full intimidation as the innocent one is in an opened wound from where the suffering is pouring out. Now the child is punished for having the effects of the sadistic abuse. The victim is punished for the "blood" from the "wound". The raped girl is now prosecuted for the "wound" inflicted by the sadists. More when there is a scar, the sadists demand that the innocent be exposed so that others see it. In many cases, sadists can even say – look, we are taking care of the innocent one now, and the innocent then is under cohesive control for what? For the reactivation from the inflicted sadism. Please see it. We have such communities, organisations, and institutions all over the world. They intervene sadistically towards the innocent person's life and surveillance this person while stealing this person's precious knowledge (and gaining a profit on it, anyway). These organisations rise on this kind of sadistic crimes – on somebodies legacy and intelligence while to cover this – sadists will call the innocent one "an idiot" as the idiot now is bleeding... and they will comment how much the idiot can be so stupid to bleed from the "wounding" and again the innocent one is under interrogation and cohesive control. And merry-go-round...

As a sadistic strategic abuse, exposure is coming based on toxic shame. The victim is shown publicly under to do not know why...? under sadistic persecution – the victim is shown with this scar what was done frankly to the child, not the other way around. To the child – as a person under psychological tortures under prolongation lands in a place of infantilisation, what is the next step of sadistic strategic abuse. So, in this case, the innocent one – the child is now marked as someone "less than" – as the innocent is "bleeding" – which again is giving relief to the perpetrator. Remember, the perpetrator makes money (or profit, for example, creates a new job position) on it – on the cost of the life of the innocent one, on the money of the innocent one. I would have a worldwide career till now if sadistic strategic abuse was not done on me by thousands of sadists in my life. It's a relational field made by sadist from power over the victim (innocent one does not crave masochism as it's never about masochism – bigger explanation is in *I Will Tell, Anyway!*) – this can happen in the sadistic family system, sadistic community system, sadistic educational system. All cultures can be sadistic, and no one will see it – as will take it as a norm, and now we have whole sadistic nations with some innocent individuals left in there somewhere who till now did not take their own life by suicide, somehow...

Let's say if the child would feel that it is love, that this way the child is important to the parent – by being belittled. If the child would feel a true love on this limited accessible pattern in a child created by the sadistic family system (and if this would create the "safety" in this child – relational sadistic fields called by the sadists "teasing"), then the child would understand that this is not threat (but a norm). Let's see this as a cause and an effect. While the rest of the sadistic family system is interested in observation and learning from the child being abused sadistically, all the collective is arising to the level of sadistic strategic abuse. Cause – sadism through psychological tortures, effect – suffering is seen as unconscious actions and reactivation (what if rather real blood we have here an addiction in the innocent? The innocent one cannot breathe under sadism, cannot have their own life under sadism, and from this, all play they go onto disconnection and in most cases harm themselves through addictive behaviour). Again – the innocent one is created as the biggest problem for the sadists. Now we have addicted, disconnected, suffering one who is made a problem by the sadistic system (remember – the sadistic system itself is a huge problem and never ever the innocent one) – the same story with "bleeding" – now is the persecution of being addicted, etc. The sadistic system would never admit "how come we could make such a mistake?" as this would undermine their non-existent 'smartness' they believe they have as sadistic societies and moreover "people watch us," so what now? It would shake all the system itself.

Sadistic games have no end. Sadists will try to withhold all the information about themselves and their addictions, their own addiction to control and crimes as cohesive control on the innocent is a criminal action. Even spreading lies about the innocent is a criminal action as it's a slander, and under the law, it's a crime. So look at this again – now the innocent one is going to be punished for the 'crying' literal one, or now the literal one – is going to be prosecuted for the effect. So the persecution or in the sadistic family system or in the sadistic institutional system – this innocent one now as being a problem is the one who is causing all of it – so now starts blame – maybe even the innocent one is blamed for being "hysterical" under CIA interrogation? No, No, No, it's not a human - human never ever is under reactivation from inflicted psychological tortures. So the innocent under sadistic tortures should stop – it's the desired power over for the sadists – and the innocent nervous system is fully dysregulated, and the innocent one now is fully traumatised the way it happened to me in Australia – no, there was no harassment.

Under full traumatisation, all the body is under dysregulation and reactivation and is fully possessed by the sadists – and this is what they want from the innocent person. The innocent should hide now to survive while is simply literally or not "choking" in "reactivation" and is almost eaten inside with the pain and suffering totally left alone.

EXPOSURE for Punishment/Persecution

Exposure of the victim in suffering is full enjoyment for the sadists. They don't see the innocent person as a human, as the sadist is not a human. It's a show where it is a disaster. In this disaster, the child or innocent they are victims, but indeed the sadist is the one who is the shameful disaster which is imputing the disaster onto an innocent. The sadist sees the child as a targeted object, a product for production, a tool for usage to have an emotional show for the sadists' hidden agenda. What is seen as a sadistic show is all about the innocent, but remember – everything that is shown is about the sadists. To show this more clearly, it's like the sadist is using the innocent person as their own EXTENSION – so all who observe – they see the innocent on the front-line – the child in misery – BUT this is the sadist who is in misery and is imputing this onto the child. Sadist also involves their sexual energy in it – so is using the innocent person's sexuality or sexual topics to charge on it. There is sexual attraction based on usage, anyway, from the parent to the child or from the sadistic partner/person to the innocent person. Sadist shames publicly for no reason. If there are no reasons, sadist will invent the reasons based on toxic lies. The child, of course, doesn't understand this because children are not interested in sex on a certain stage of development, so they don't understand this intensity and the interaction. The innocent person is manipulated with ambiguity and naturally does not get what happens if the manipulations involve sadistic strategies.

This sadistic game is done from behind that the innocent does not understand, and the sadists play this game as long as the sadist can gain the profit of what is power over and sexual release from their own tension and misery. The more reactivity is from the innocent one, the more amusement the sadist feels – it's a sexual charge on the other – it's sexual sadistic abuse. And when the child has a reaction as cannot believe, let's say that is not loved by the parent, the child starts crying. The more the innocent cries, the more empowerment and power over the sadist feels. A sadist is not capable of compassion at any single moment. Not at the beginning of the game, not in the middle of the game, and not at the end of the game. The innocent one is weaker and weaker until there is zero protection for their vulnerability, anyway. There is a child lying on the floor who is fully suffering and is in this alone – what again is the next strategy of the sadists. To keep innocent one away from real life and to keep innocent one only for themselves.

Scandal and Sadistic Amusement With its Participants

One of the strategic sadistic abuse is also public scandal used by sadists, the more public scandal, the better. The perpetrator will portray the victim in negativity even if this negativity is totally not the victim's but rather the perpetrator's negativity as the sadist will use the victim to show their own negativity through the passage – which is, for them, the victim itself. This is happening because the sadist has no eyes to see the victim – who the innocent person is – this person is never seen – never. Sadistic eyes see only an inner mirror of sadism – what they say from their own sadistic zoom. Sadist 'truth' as sadistic lies are now shown in the worst possible scenarios, which naturally is destroying the innocent person's reputation what is causing naturally a ripple effect of destroying all the areas of the victim's life, including devastation, for example of, the workplace area, not mentioning any credibility area that the innocent one has no place to earn money anymore. Like one of them came to me when I was crying and said, "Ewa, I want to help you" what ended up for me with such deep exploitation on any possible level that, in fact, till today, I did neither receive payment for this offered work nor credit for it under my name as my own authorship for the inventions. Does this sound familiar to you?

Sadistic strategic abuse is based on sadistic jealousy (sadistic jealousy has destruction, healthy jealousy has future promotional visions that are up levelling the observer from the inside). There was never a sadistic scandal not based on sadistic jealousy and envy. Sadistic jealousy of a sadistic person or sadistic community has fundamentals on sadistic toxic shame inside of their sadistic beholder/s. Sadists feel small that is why they are so "vulnerable" on a jealousy level. So this way, our world lost till now so many hard-working genuine, vulnerable people/genius who became an innocent victim of the sadist/s. Observing such a market based on the sadistic scandal – the profit has the hidden one and naturally is 'not' their negativity (conscious/unconscious negativity of sadistic beholder) on the flashlights. While it's exactly their negativity on the innocent one now marked somehow (remember sadists choose victim for their extension what means unconsciously they lay out their projections onto the innocent one who now imprisoned by sadists shines the sadists' exposed negativity – the sadist inside). Sadist uses their power over for certain profit, if not for sadistic show amusement (someone is up, someone is down), then for the sadistic usage.

I was in the city centre near the central shops area around two years ago. One woman was cached as she was probably 'stealing' in one of the clothes shops. The guard grabbed her quickly and almost brought out of the shop like a dog on a leash. They were waiting for the police. The guardian took an opportunity to take advantage of her. He started abusing her in front of the people walking through the shop's hall.

I looked at his face – as all was happening quite fast – on his face was amusement and some kind of power over that he is squeezing her hands behind her body, behind her, more down and down. While he was pushing her hands more from down now towards up and up, she bent in a very short time more and more. Her bottom was now exposed. People who were nearby, they stopped, and around 10 people started recording her on their cell phones. I was standing there in some kind of shock. The guardian was in amusement all this time while his amusement hit the pick point when her bottom was exposed. And for all the observers, obviously...

"the theft was caught." But why the guard is using his power over her while she is not even moving to run away, more she is silent and passive... The whole sadistic show is recorded. All observers recording her without consent have mostly all of them smile on their faces. Some talk to each other and laugh. Do they see the abuse, or do they justify that the woman is punished – or publicly prosecuted...?

Let's see this closer. First, we don't know why this happens and what really happens there. All the observers see only a guardian who just called the police, and the "theft" – a woman – is bent in half with her bottom exposed. All smile and all record her. We have no idea about her actions in the shop at all. We all see only part of it – the motif while remembering as per childhood restrictions that the theft is a crime (let's say from an educational perspective, some have this in their head as judgers...). Obviously, no one sees her as a human. We don't know anything about her. Maybe she was not stealing at all. For example, maybe the guardian just wanted to use his power over the woman. More, no one will prove it when the police will come here. Why? Because the guardian has authority. And what about her motif. Maybe she is a theft, maybe she is not aware of stealing, maybe she is addicted to stealing, or maybe she was stealing something for her kids as she is poor, maybe she has no work after running away from the domestic violence house, maybe she was thrown away by her family after she was raped and shamefully excluded from family because of the rape as it's a shame for this family outside face. Maybe she has cancer, and she is not working for months, and it's already close to winter, and she simply felt it was too cold for her and she had no money, and in her understanding, maybe that was not a big deal. And it's not any of explanations to the place of if there was stealing or not. What if... when she was in the wardrobe shop changing her clothes he was trying to rape her and then when she wanted to escape he grabbed her and the piece of the clothes she was checking – and this way from his shame and rejection place he is using his place as a workplace area to accuse her of being theft of these piece of clothes. What then? Less a possible scenario? Well.. why this woman is so passive and does not fight? Why is this woman not talking at all? It can be hard to believe, but she could be in shock after shock trauma when she was a child and her father, each time she was changing clothes, was raping her as an opportunity matched for him, and in the shop, this just happens again. And what if her father said, "If you tell anyone, I will kill you," for example?

The main place of talk in here is that the observers do not know anything that really happens – they are all out of context – only seeing the aftermath, and all are in sadistic amusement. We don't know anything about her. We as observers see only the observation in now... moreover, for whose NOW? So let's continue. What is happening in this situation truly what the observers see in 'now' is the guardian as an authority, who is using power over the other human who is not attacking and is in a passive state with her hands twisted at her back. In contrast, her hands are being hanged upper and upper. What we see in 'now' as observes the guardian is abusing her this way, trapping her even more and more – remember she is a centre of attention in this, and no one knows she is in shock... and her mouth is locked by invisible key. After a while, she gives a sign of feeling pain through her facial expression. Now, all who record her on the cell phone are in even bigger amusement. "What a funny face" – someone from the crowd laughs at her, now more people start laughing, and her red face from pain and shame is now viral online. She is obviously dehumanised publicly and humiliated in this moment of physical entrapment. Frankly, those who are recording it without her consent and putting this on social media are also committing crimes (remember – they see her as a criminal! Isn't this a paradox?). She is punished publicly already for...? She is a public victim who is under sadistic persecution of hearing others laughing at her. She feels overpowered and entrapped. Now we have all criminals – a woman who was stealing – if she was really "stealing" or "stealing" was happening to her? Please give time for yourself to see this. Here is also a guardian who is abusing her sadistically and the observers who are abusing her also. All the show is a place of sadism, and all are sadistic criminals – yes! Exactly sadistic criminals soaking like parasites on an innocent woman as the truth was... the guardian wanted to rape her in the wardrobe area...

Let's see further – who will be punished when the police finally come? The woman? Probably yes. Why? If there are no shop recordings and anything she took away – she will be left free – really, will she be left (and what if the guardian is always calling the same police "friend"?). Wasn't it a sexual assault what the guardian did, including recording perpetrators? A collective crime. More, when the police come, and there is proof, she will be punished for what she has done while no one will ever be punished for what was done to her. The guardian is taking advantage of this situation, and the people who record her also.

Let's see this a bit further... what if the guardian and the policeman know each other and are friends? And they have had this kind of sadistic game for years on innocent clients? What if we see a bit farther that the policeman is taking her with him to the car, but they do not go to the police office with the victim? What is happening under sadistic strategic abuse when the sadist will take the victim personally? Remember, she's doing nothing. There is no humanity in all the show. First, all situation is seen out of context. Second, all the situation is focused on one person. Third, some observers take all situations personally, including the guardian... and maybe the policeman.

Remember – personal issues are always a problem for the person who feels the personal issue inside themselves. It's not a problem for the targeted object, no matter what. What is happening – let's see closer – she's not running away. She is just waiting for the police while being a victim of sadistic group abuse. She seems passive and almost like agreeing with the situation she is in. The guardian abuses her with sadistic power over, including amusement.

Under sadistic strategic abuse in many societies where is used as a tool power over we can observe this clearly in sadistic psychiatric hospitals, in sadistic therapy fields as sadistic therapeutical associations, in sadistic communities and in sadistic family systems. It's not the one who makes crimes – if truly makes them and if is not manipulated that is doing them rather the sadist, while it is the whole system which makes crimes on one innocent! Why is it not seen like this? Well, who could believe!?

Eyes of the Sadistic Beholder

So what does it look like from the eyes of the beholder? It's a totally different picture from the perspective of the sadist and from the victim's perspective, also will be different from the perspective of the observers, as previously mentioned. The crying object is now punished. The wounded person is "bleeding" and is prosecuted for this. What if we talk about the person who reports a rape, more if this person is a child or teenager and reports the abuse? In most societies and communities, including higher instances all over the world, this is the victim's responsibility for what happened – no, not the perpetrator's responsibility for what happened, and the innocent one will be punished for this. When I came back home fully traumatised after being in Australia, I asked one person who would take responsibility for what happened to me there as sadism. The answer was – "You, Ewa – you, Ewa, will take responsibility for what happened to you." And I took, I started the healing process. My question is, who took responsibility for destroying my life sadistically?

The victim is sadistically abused even more, mocked and dehumanised more and more. Sadists know what they are doing, not taking responsibility and ownership for the sadistic crimes. They lash out with hatred at a vulnerable person – and start inflicting punishment and pointing at the victim. It's a strategy – and tragedy for the victim. The more the sadist can give punishment, the more the sadist feels power over – through control of the punishment and coercive control. For the sadists, all is a fuel to exist on the innocent one as on the extension – it's parasite extension. It's for them almost a blood in the veins and air in the lungs – imputing sadism onto the innocence and laughing at their victim who is "bleeding" now. And they pump themselves from their smallness. They very strictly hide from all the world and live in lies while feeling some relief that the other person's life was destroyed and not theirs. So the report of the sadistic abuse is done now. The sadistic family system or sadistic community now will try to hide the shown sadisms, as it is shining on the whole system! Remember, the sadistic system/society/community do not want to show their sadisms and usage of the one participant. They even earn money on the fixed – based on the more "bleeding" person, the more sadistic profit.

So what is happening with the child later after being punished for the effect of the sadistic abuse? The child feels entrapped and is like bottled where the gas is in buzzing. The child inhibits all reactivation after all from the games of the sadist, which are imputed in prolongation – it's like a dance – the reactivation in a victim is the ignition of all this domino. Remember, the innocent one is the most healthy among all the sadistic systems. With the adult is the same, while the person who came through such sadistic games from their own perpetrators in childhood, the adult as an innocent one will have the same amount of triggers which are bottled unfortunately on the same level of buzzing. When the opening happens – pouring out from the wound appears as a simple reactivation based on trauma. A sadist is the one who judges it. It's important to dismantle that reactivation on trauma differs from reactivation as a reaction to abuse. The second one can be a healthy, not developed pattern, for example, in a teen, but it's not trauma. Resentment, for example, in the innocent one, does not have to be a trauma at all but rather a way of showing that there was a boundary rupture.

Under sadistic strategic abuse, the innocent one is thrown towards the circle for the reactivation in themselves. No one wants to take responsibility for this. Definitely not the sadists and not the sadistic community or family / sadistic institutional system. The innocent one stops crying and looks like death now – all is inhibited again. It's a closed box, and this is this program, the innocent one infantilised by the sadistic system (as the most healthy among all of the sadists) or NOT! is carrying all their entire life unconsciously creating the same relational field with the others, not seeing that again and again there are only sadists.

So what happened with me under strategic sadistic

abuse? It was mostly a sadistic scandal show based on sexual sadistic energy to show "who I am – as a sadistic show "About 'me', without me" in it at all. I was falsely accused on and on and on – I was accused of harassment by a group of people in women's bodies while the reality is I was not accused of harassment, more there was no harassment – they were harassing themselves in the sadistic show and me in it being harassed additionally by them. That was a false accusation based on nothing, and frankly, later on, when I read this message, it was only a warning, not even an accusation. What is the warning built inside of the sadists – it's a warning based on their eyes of the sadistic beholder. Can be destroyed innocent person life by the sadistic eyes of sadistic beholders? Yes can be – my own life is an example. And it can happen if the sadists are in the majority and the innocent one is ONE and left alone when the sadist represents white supremacy and has access to some levels of authority over and the innocent does not, and when the innocent is 'bleeding' from traumatisation and the sadists naturally and obviously not – and the innocent one is now the biggest problem of all the sadistic community or even sadistic nation.

The person who put me into this traumatic threat based on life/death reactivation and onto highly stressed situation – it was a sadistic strategy as it is not based on my safety – no, it is based on the sadist's safety (*I Will Tell, Anyway!* by Ewa Lawresh). Strategy is hanging a vulnerable person on the other side, later on 'hanged by the tongue' – while using the opportunity that I am in a place of full trauma reactivation and opened half-mutism. So later, unconsciously, this created even bigger trauma from a place of vulnerability than before. This reaction from the relational field of me-sadists reactivated the unconscious program in me from childhood created by sadists in the sadistic family system and later all the communities/ organisations/institutions/groups. From the place of full threat that I will die – to the place of dependency and intimidation also in the way that my car was constantly broken and the message "We don't want you here" – sadists evoked in me my childhood trauma based on the received previously detailed information. It was strategic and fully planned, but I didn't know this. Me as a victim in Australia attacked by a group of people, this all reactivated all the adversity from early childhood till throughout my life – the sadistic – innocence attachment (never masochist, as it's a child, as well the child is not interested in sadism, as well, is not interested in sex). That was all recreated from reactivated traumatised nervous system. As all was planned, so all was sadistically observed. As all was sadistically observed, everyone could take part in taking advantage of me at any time, as everything was sadistically planned. Then taken advantage of me was also sadistically observed. Then the sadism was even deeper as those who sadistically observed – no one came to tell me that I am under strategic sadistic abuse. No one told me directly what is happening. More, they all charged on me and my life. Would you like to know what would happen if I knew what was happening sadistically behind my back? I would commit suicide, yes as many till today commit suicide for group mockery and group bullying, so what can we say when there is a sadistic collective plan and all laugh sadistically but do not inform me about it (I only see their laughter at)? Yes, innocent people take their own life – they take it from a rebel place or harm themselves from a rebel place. If some are lucky, they will transmute it onto something healthy as a rebel – while there is still pain and suffering from sadistic strategic abuse. I am not mentioning here about the second group – the sadists. They are not innocent.

So all distress created back then was a degradation (making someone small and worse than others even for the sake of the whole community as an "exposed piece of meat as a front-line trash bin" for the sadists in this place is easier to go on living, the exposed has to struggle being left alone and symbolically the innocent one is now publicly "bandaged" and "hanged" with zero consent – remember this) of innocent human being and I was weaken and weaken more and more. That means the person who is in this place is vulnerable on any possible level because the protective layer is totally removed. It's happening by the shock, which creates full intimidation based on a life/death threat. So I was punished for my reactivity, judged and laughed at for the effect of traumatisation in prolongation based on unpredictable shocks. Now I was exposed to my vulnerability, and now I was exposed fully without any safety and protection – to sadism from anyone who wished to participate.

Chapter 8

Sadistic Dance Around HER Face

False FACE of the Sadists – the Outside Reputation as a Visible Etiquette

Sadists are most scared of losing their fake face – they hide behind sadistic community / system / organisation. They use power over to protect their fake face. The face is for them important because they have their reputation based on this fake "face." It's a structural picture of complex essentials in one small body. Sadistic social justice is blind about that as well as social workers. These all sadists use power over the innocent, and they will do everything to cover any negativity about themselves and their community. In contrast, they will do everything to expose the innocent about the traits exactly the sadists themselves are hiding. Paradox? Negativity exposure is now public about the innocent (even if it's not about innocent at all) but not about the whole sadistic community. They hide, and they use control for this. Shining light onto the victim's negativity is helpful for them for few reasons. It's very essential for the sadists that the innocent one will never ever gain public/social respect. This way, sadists destroy through lies and later through gossip about innocent person public 'face' and later create social rejection. In most cases, an innocent person commits suicide. For the majority, public rejection is on the levels of physical pain. Those who do not care about their public 'face' the ones who are brave remain alive (like, for example, me). But remember, the one who is destroying an innocent person's public 'face' is the one who is scared the most to lose it.

Let's see this closer. What sadist is the most scared of is losing the outside face as so called 'reputation.' No one knows who the sadist is privately or behind the 4 walls, but the sadist has been building this so-called 'reputation' for a long time. This construct is a tool for manipulating the public arena and industry/work area. Sadist is scared the most to see who they are inside that is why their fingers are always in the majority towards themselves – it's like they cannot hide it. Unfortunately, most people don't see these pictures hidden behind a layer of 'reputation' and fake authority because of the 'reputation'. Sometimes this so called 'reputation' is also a wrapped up group of people in one community forming a sadistic community and this way forming a whole bunch of wrapped up outside 'reputation'. This 'reputation' is needed to benefit in society as a usage of innocence.

One is that they gain false "pureness" by showing the targeted problem as it brings sadistic unseen societal attention towards the victim – by CONTRAST. Negative one single problem and Positive all the society. Society is conditioned that it's not the community that is drastically unhealthy and fully sadistic. Still, it's the innocent one who is their scapegoat – a front-line shield (where is written by the sadist! "Pour on her," "Vomit on her," "Born being a trash bin, here you can throw YOUR garbage"). Within the braces of the sadistic community, they can do with victims whatever they want. They can choose their victims for certain sadistic usage. For example, if their marriage is not working from the place of – the sadist and the victim – the sadist will choose the next victim to blame that their marriage is falling apart because of the victim, but the sadist will never ever admit publicly that this is the sadist who is destroying their own marriage as per the partner does not want to take part in this sadistic dance. The next targeted object will be chosen to cover the falling apart marriage that at least all can see that it's not the sadist's part that this is the way it is – it is because of the third party of course (this party is an innocent person mostly do not even know is chosen to be involved even in this false accusation as it's behind their back). So its strategic sadistic abuse and public face is very much needed for them. They spread attention toward the target, and this way, they do not lose their fake face publicly. So it's essential to observe who still keeps their positive image while the innocent is under sadistic psychological tortures – who is the hidden one and not seen in the public arena and is taking it all, including profit? Under psychological tortures, the tortured child or innocent person is normally not observed as a victim and targeted object who is a human and has a character, their own life experiences and simply blood under the skin, but is seen through the eyes of sadistic communities. The innocent one is the one who is falsely accused. The person is in need and looking for help and becomes an even bigger scapegoat than was made before. It's never a choice, neither physical rape nor psychological rape.

When the innocent one admits – yes, I was raped, yes, this was a rape – unfortunately, it's a trap in the face of sadists. So it means there is no possibility to express the truth as sadists are turning upside down everything that was said. We can observe such sadistic dynamics from sadistic social justice, sadistic systems in hospitals, and sadistic work areas with sadistic disconnections based on sadistic bonding, including sadistic domestic violence. The victim is under reactivation, can be laying on the floor and screaming while from the perspective, let say, of the walker on the street, as an observer, can wonder what is it happening with this person and what this person is doing on the floor, more – why is this person screaming? And now starts judgement. Judgement belongs to two groups of people – those who sleep (are not aware and are not in now and are not educated and are innocent) and to those who are sadists.

The next thought would be that the person should be now locked in a psychiatric hospital. This is all about unhealthy (can be sadistic) observer. Sadists will feel amusement and sadistic joy and will even record the person on their cell phone and put this on social media. While the healthy observer will feel compassion and at least start a "helping process." What happens if the observers are people of power over like sadistic guardians, sadistic police, or sadistic gurus? An innocent cannot be seen as a human who is suffering but rather as a targeted object. For the victim under suffering to become the targeted object, this can even more, traumatise the victim. So public face is needed for the perpetrator as they can manipulate the scapegoat and also controlling the scapegoat through public face without the scapegoat in it at all! Can you imagine?

When I was a child, we played on the ground and walked on the street an elderly woman. She suddenly fell down and hit the ground with her face. I was with a group of children, and we were playing nearby. Her face was lying on the cement platform, bleeding. Her face was fully red from the blood. She was passively lying on the floor, with no movement. She seemed to be in shock, and her face seemed very strange and scary from the child's perspective, at least in my child's eyes. I felt compassion while I was in shock myself about what did just happen. And her face was no longer the same face when the person was walking. And I remember when all the children from the playground stopped playing and started laughing at her. I was the only one among them all who was not laughing. And I remember me being in shock observing now all group of children laughing at her, pointing fingers and laughing again, talking to each other and again laughing at her. She was maybe 70 years old. From time to time, there was some movement in her, like shaking and like she wanted to say something, but it was some voice which could be not understood. It was not clear spelling. I was standing there and not laughing. I was maybe 8 years old, standing there in shock. The rest of the kids were somewhere around my age. And I was asking myself what was such funny seeing a woman with a red face laying on the floor near the street, bleeding? In these kids, is already inner sadism reactivated.

The question is, did these children lose their sense of humanity? What is happening in these children's nervous system when they laugh at her that they are capable of having fun and enjoyment and do not feel at least compassion? What did their eyes see that was so funny about this bleeding woman?

A few years ago I was travelling by bus, and while I was sitting in one line, on the left side, on my right side there was sitting a woman and closer to the window there was sitting a boy, maybe 6 years old. Just suddenly, from her bag, she took out the sandwich – the double sliced bread with a lot of ingredients, quite huge with salad. Next of her move was the first hit on the child's mouth with the sandwich that he took a bite of it as big as he could. She did not give the sandwich to the child's hands. She was hitting with it into his mouth, faster and faster. All was happening very, very fast for me as an observer, and I was surprised if what was happening was real. And so, with such impact, the child started choking and crying while his head was pushed into the window, but she didn't stop. She was continuously doing it again. He was choking more and more. After my intervention, she finally stopped. It was her sadism.

We have to understand that sadism and psychological tortures are entrapment of innocent people. What was done towards this child was obviously sadism, including dehumanisation, belittling and violation of human freedom and human rights and treating a child as a targeted object of relief – for sadism. For this woman in a bus, obviously, this child was not a human who feels. It was like an object onto which the sandwich could be pushed through as much as she could. Unfortunately, children will do everything to be loved, and they will rather stop loving themselves instead stop loving the sadist. So this is a relational trap based on survival. While as you see from these two examples, kids are also behaving differently – some can laugh at somebody's misery and tragedy, which is a real trauma for the victim, and some can be entrapped on the other site – as being an innocent victim. Who are you in these two stories? One of the strategies is to cover who the sadist is while this is the sadist who is hanging the victim publicly. While the society, unfortunately, sees only the victim and gives negative reviews, let's say online again, only about the victim. It's the virtual world of the sadists – virtual, which means not real. They can even simulate the effects in the victim's brain. When the victim is fully traumatised, record the victim, or report the victim to put the victim to an institution like a psychiatric hospital/under surveillance/to prison or put under cohesive control, anyway... Sadists nicely represent outside their organisation, showing how polite they are on the street while nobody knows what the person is truly keeping behind the home's walls. A group of sadists is a powerful seduction place for the victim. They invite to destroy. And there is a sadistic plan, even yearly planned they are after all empowered in sadistic abuse.

If for once you would see this from a different

perspective, let say for example it's World War II, 1943, summer, and people in the camp can walk outside only to the small centre – in a small city where live people who do not know that there is a World War II. At the same time, there are people who are in army clothes – prosecutors from the camps – while now they are with their families walking on the same streets. They are all passing each other – when the citizens of this city are in it, aren't involved, they only see a walking person under trauma and a walking person in army clothes – in this case. Observers judge as the picture with components does not match the life they lead. No one sees the tortures, and no one sees the person under the tortures at the exact moment. In these circumstances, they only see the outcome – two walking characteristics – a thin traumatised person in freeze and a smiling in amusement person in army clothes.

Object of Destruction – Face – Sexism, Misogyny, Misandry

Sadistic strategic abuse is based on object destruction and object degradation because, for the sadists, a human is not a human. It's an object of manipulation – it's an enslaved person for exploitation that sadists can raise their sadistic communities and business on object's suffering and can do everything what they want with the object through inflicting pain under psychosocial tortures. So now they can manipulate the public image of the suffering object, put false accusations, harass and accuse of harassment, stalk and accuse of stalking – it's like they, in a rapistic way, penetrate the object all this time. What is happening under real physical rape indeed because this is not a woman for them – it's an object (many sadists will even change her gender behind her back to inflict rapes and cruelty better). This is only an object and only an object. It's not somebody who can be treated beautifully with a huge grace and respect as simply for being a human. They turn it into the place that she has to obey being from now on under cohesive control (explained as for "a higher matter" or "for her good") while building careers on her.

No, there is no my man version as let's say, for example, John – I was born as a girl, and I identify as a cisgender straight woman. Though to the surprise of the whole sadistic societies, everyone on this planet carries inside as a union – wholeness – feminine and masculine energy. I have never had gender issues, and I have never had pussy issues. Though sadists probably, as a projection of who they are, had this phobia about themselves. As well, as we possess inside feminine and masculine energy, also we as well are capable of loving not on a bodily level but on a soul level. This, again, has no influence on changing me behind my back as a form of backstabbing from Lady to Gentleman. Sadists operate on the level of meat, etiquettes, labels, and titles, and as the objectification of the targeted object – the human is not a human for them – it's only an object to manoeuvre. In this place steps into the arena of sadistic infantilisation as a sadist's limitations of being a box. This way, swinging on the past line is not possible for the sadists because statists see the object, so they manoeuvre on the level of the spot, but zero swinging. If they form groups – to keep calm within insinuated ambiguity – which is part of the highest forms of art – sadists go from confusion to blowing out. That is why control is so much important for the sadists. They operate on control – they are addicted to the control. They must to go to the treatment centres to heal addictions from control (inner 'controlism' vs inner 'alcoholism') and power over (this way, fingers pointing in the majority are truthfully showing the addicted societies in a place of one small girl as a scapegoat vs all sadistic societies).

Sexism is an operational centre for sadistic communities as a form of repressed inner hidden controlism exposed with the rapistic culture onto the scapegoat.

I got pregnant and said to one of my perpetrators that I could not work in this area anymore for the time of my pregnancy. The perpetrator threatened me with prolongation throughout all my pregnancy that I would pay for refusing – as one of the biggest fears of sadists is being rejected (from their grandiose perspective, "How come you dare to reject me?!"). Sadists possess the innocent one – at least they are convinced about it in themselves for themselves. Sadists hatred rejection and will lash out with any possible lie towards the victim and false accusations against the victim.

Now consider when you see the Lady:

Is it easier to believe in her as being a man's version than admit public misogyny and find justification for the violence on a woman's body on any possible level, including usage of image and copyrighted materials (for, let's say, symbolic sadistic arousal/sadistic revenge)? Is it easier to believe in her as being a man's version and admit public misandry and find justification for the violence on a woman's body on any possible level, including false accusations around harassment which have never had a place (for let's say symbolic face destruction/physical market removal)?

FACE FACE FACE

What have sadists done with my "face"? Why do sadists love destroying human face publicly?

I am where I am not, I am not where I am. If I am in the sadist's head, I am not there. In the sadist's head is only sadism – from this place are formed false sadistic accusations. That means in the sadist's head is a sadist, not me – from this place, the sadist accuses the other about who the sadist is. So, in fact, all accusations from the sadist's face are accusations about the sadist themselves.

Sadism is about life/death threats and intimidation. Then the sadist feels empowered, and the smile on the sadist's face is the same exaggerated in a caricature like the red face of the victim – all to exaggerate everything, to make the show much more exposed and drastically going under the skin of the observer – for the sadistic amusement and/or for the intimidation matters. One of the intimidating me under sadism was that once I received threats that "We will take your skin off," that they will "burn me alive that there only dress will remain," so to such extent that I would be left as only a skeleton wearing a dress. Another threat was that "You will pay for all the humanity" as mentioned before. Direct threats from sadists were "I will destroy your life," "I will take care of your life that you have no human rights," "You will lose all human rights," and more, more such level sentences. Inflicting psychological tortures is the basement of all the strategies of sadistic strategic abuse. This means psychological tortures are not seen as per se as torture as no one can report it the same as physical torturers. They are simply not seen by the outside observer, let's say institutional judger and cult prosecutor. What the observer sees, though, is only the reaction of the tortured innocent one. So all that is the aftermath. And now sadists come to the highest pick point (they sell fixated rigid ways of living on the innocence without consent out of context, on the cost of innocence without consent, on innocence's vitality and on innocence's life energy [this what kidnappers do with innocent kids, as well what did happen to me in my childhood, btw] or any other fixated strategies about nervous system or fixing the stolen 'car' parts) – they get the pick show – observed situation out of context.

Let's see this closer:

A raped girl, skirt torn, wounds between legs, blood on her tights, she is asking for the direction where is the closets police office as her cell phone was stolen under rape – observer out of context on the other side of the street sees it and thinks "a dirty whore who is approaching a teen" –

while at this moment comes the other one to the observer and say – "I know her, she was a prostitute years ago" – the observer responded surprised now – "Really?" The other observer says – "No, I am joking," and leaves the show. The first observer still observes – but an observer is a man who was abused by a woman in childhood who was touching him sexually on his thighs. He sees the thighs – he feels trauma for a moment, and he accuses this innocent girl on the street who is asking for help in the directions of the police office – this observer is accusing her out of context for the attempt that she is harassing a teen boy on the street. WOW WOW WOW, now we have a messssssss... What is the continuation?

The observer feels so triggered that calls the police. He sees in the teen boy himself (btw, the teen who is helping our raped innocent one is searching for the closest police office on the online maps). The observer is reporting the innocent woman, and what now!? Police are coming. They jump on the girl from nowhere and attack her from behind. She is now laying on the floor, just raped by a man, now raped by a group of men... what a show... Now we have a group of sadists, let's say, for example, middle-class social workers, who are crossing the street. They just finished their sadistic power over the innocent – social work – why sadistic? – as they hate their own job. Remember – it's still an example. One of the sadistic social workers says, "It's good for her," "Fuc*king whore approaching teen boys," "You fuc*king whore!"

Imagine this innocent one on the floor being under rape

again hears this... and she remembers the words of her father now... the same cement floor in the basement, the same cold floor she feels when the policeman is squeezing her head to the floor that she cannot move it. She tries to breathe, she was just raped, she almost forgot about the initial rape from before the 30 min ago, now she remembers only her father and his hands on her face and the sentences "You fuc*king whore."

Social justice women feel justice, feel pride, and walk away in amusement and contempt – "Yes, this woman on the floor will get her 'justice'."

The teen boy is in shock – he has now reactivated his half mutism – cannot even explain what really happens in here – police are asking him questions, and what he can do, he is only showing his cell phone – the police open the page and what sees? The searching of police office...

Wow, wow, wow – now police man says to the teen boy – as he also has a son – "Be a strong boy," "We will take care of the situation, now you are safe, come back home." Teen is in shock and cannot speak... he wishes to explain but is in shock, and his face is showing this as he is visibly stunned by what has really happened. For him personally, all is happening so fast as he saw his mom on the floor after his mom was raped... he feels dizzy now... he wants to help the woman as it's his mom... now...

Look, now let's say we add people who hatred the woman on the floor – more and more observers are here and there, and more of them are starting recording her. Some just pass it, it's an interesting show, and some are excited from inner sadism.

What would happen if now, just by accident, there was walking her ex? Or her boss, who hatred her so so much that the only dream is to destroy her private and public face – well, he says "She is so loyal to me" in hypocrisy speaking...

Now the video is online... her squeezed face is online...

Hate starts from here.

What about the stolen cell phone of our raped girl? Maybe they even will invent all the story of the above the way that the rapist who stole the cell phone of this girl was the one from her company – to get the invention she just invented, which can be sold for billions. Well, now the story looks a bit different – as we have a new context – let's widen this a bit. What if one of the policemen is a friend of her ex-boyfriend who is selling her for fixated rigid ways of living, for example, or for a "media project" whatever. See it... In the end, the girl lost everything, including the intimacy between legs and the billion-dollar self-brain invention. Now it's sold without her – she is in 'prison'... (real-life based on isolation) as her ex found that some fixed rigid ways of living, for example, did not sell too well... as he expected so, he invented the lies to put her there even more.

Now, what about the people who took part in this show, each one of them – and those who took the innocent woman personally? And who had naturally power over her – she was the one on the floor, she was the one who was just raped, she was the one who had no voice, she was the one... who was accused of harassment and molestation of the teen boy who in fact wants to help her from the early beginning but now is himself in huge shock and dissociation. She, while lying on the floor, is also in dissociation... and now she thinks "How could my dad do this to me? He is supposed to love me and protect me..." she feels no protection now... no...

How long can we go in this story? What if we spread this onto the globe so that everyone will take part... well, almost everyone...

Personally... my heart goes to this innocent woman on the street... SHE IS INNOCENT!

Sadism... if we let sadism rule now, she laying on the floor maybe will be used to "help" someone to sell some 'fixated rigid ways of living a life' – which has nothing to do with a human who is a river and constant flow. Who has control over the situation? Who has human rights in here...? If we put onto this situation, one lost component – PREJUDICE! What would happen then?

The end of the story is that the innocent woman is asking if she will get global compensation and recompensate after what happened to her, her mind, body, brain, nervous system, image, her energy, her tights, her face... will she have human rights ever again...? Who does say it? Who does lead it? Who is monitoring it? Who is the one about decision making in here? Does this one is really entitled to decide who I am? No, there is no place to ask her – "What happened to her?" now she is the accused one! And now she "will pay for all the humanity" – can you imagine??? What a story...

I am very serious in this book as sadistic strategic abuse is real. In many cults and communities, people are killed this way, or they finally commit suicide from the experienced psychological tortures – and to cover it in the direction again, it will be towards the next innocent girl but not towards the whole communities/family system/ organisations/institutions/academics.

Sadists by observing the object under psychological torturers feel amusement from this reactivation – it's what matters most. More as in the example sadistic social workers have already decided (btw not all social workers are sadistic, some may have compassion, but most are abusing their power over the innocent) to give themselves the right to decide now what will happen next! Many addicted mothers are put into prison! by such sadistic social workers who are addicted themselves! Who is making decisions? Those who work in the decision making areas – police, social justice (social loves persecution), etc. And they laugh at the targeted innocent object under psychological pain – they don't know the context, sometimes they know the context but sadism is made this way – to know and to turn it around – upside down – some don't want to understand the reaction – "I am a worker of the university, I have titles in here, oh no, I am not this woman lying there on the floor in this dirty skirt."

How to understand the reaction of the targeted object while! you are only the observer? You understand it – or well... judge it from your own context. More, the more the observer is in hatred and misery and smallness in their own life – the way the object will be judged. The same way the kid is adopted. If the kid is adopted to the parents who are farmers, cannot have to become – a farmer herself. But there is an opportunity. The same way the kid adopted by the family of movie producers can become a movie producer herself – don't have to as can also become an actor or movie producer himself. More our mentioned farmer can become an actor and our movie producer can become a farmer. Context...

True Rebels Choose Themselves?

What is more important to lose your all life and don't have yourself, or to win a better life because of choosing YOURSELF and choosing healing yourself and accepting yourself from the place of compassion? Observers become judgers because they are not in a real place and a real time of what is truly happening to the targeted object. The observers are not acting under reactivation. They truly care not to be reactivated – and no, for sure, not being a rebel. Rebel in patriarchate culture is taken as a trouble one and the one who will be from now on under surveillance for years, while it's not the trouble one a pain for the community – the sadistic community is a pain for themselves and obviously for the 'trouble' one. The system is created this way and managed this way.

When the person is in safety, is not under reactivation but rather feels it is in spontaneity and natural management of energy inside. The person can be an actor and the observer at the same time, at least this is my experience, when the person reaches the place of healed any attachment with anything and then can be both at once in a place of safety, but not any more in survival. Judgers, sadistic observers who are in survival, everything that they observe, they observe inside from the patriarchal eye and judge this way. Everything is based on their beliefs, their programs and their past! If the observer who has the power over and is not actually experiencing what is experiencing the innocent one, the observer will judge. The judgement will not be based on emotions. Still, rather past triggers (intertwined with exact now to the extreme beliefs and their past) and all judgement will come from the sadistic observer's sickness connected to this trigger inside of them, in them and only in them. If they are repressed, their feelings are not 'true' emotions (rather 'information') now as these are their emotions from the past, written in the system, is triggered information – which never ever matches neither the innocent one nor the NOW – so the innocent from the now. So what sort of power has the sadistic observer if this exact observer or sadistic community has the power to make decisions about the innocent one from the place of control over and power over!? They can influence the rest of the sadists also! And the innocent one...? will be prosecuted and punished, anyway! So the observers who make decisions which are influenced onto the innocent one (who triggers them and "It's their fault" – yes, they blame the innocent one, as someone has to be blamed for the triggers in the sadists... in the sadists' opinion – but never the sadists themselves) – sadistic decisions are invaluable and harmful towards the one – towards the innocent as the system no matter what...

has to be protected within the public eye. "Others watch us – observe us." so the trash bin is created. All are now focused on the "sick" one / "crazy" one. And the rest can finally breathe...

An innocent one is always a human, and the more humanity is in an innocent one, the more innocent one is prosecuted by the sadists. Isn't this surprising? The vulnerable person is entrapped by many! And yes, we can say that everybody has the right to their own truth towards what is happening in them, WHILE at the same time they have no right for the truth about observing something from their own subjectivity based on survival.

When I was healing myself from childhood traumas and going through all developmental stages – my person was judged by the sadistic judges. My character was entirely undermined and turned upside down by all the sadists from their hatred perspective and sadistic power over based on the eye of the sadistic patriarchate beholder. Everything as a judgement you have seen about me – this was what is inside of the sadists. Yes, exactly this and all that sadists did blame you, they at the exact moment blame themselves – but the attention will be focused on the innocent one – mostly! for the matter of community/organisation – again! "Others watch us – observe us." So what do they do? From now on watch, they observe the innocent one – their made scapegoat. Sadistic, in this case, observer also is never objective as long as it is in survival. If the observer is sadistic, the judgement will be sadistic and based on sadism. If there is any personification towards the innocent one as a personal matter – the innocent one as the targeted object of the observer, that means that everything that the observer is telling – all is about the observer and resides only and only in the sadistic observer – as this crucial place is never a place of truth.

Who Takes Responsibility?

Responsibility is the last thing sadists will take. Sadists first would have to admit they are responsible for their marriage falling apart – more – they would have to admit that there was never love and that they do not love each other. Falling apart marriage is falling apart between two people not between husband's car accident or wife's lost pregnancy. Falling apart marriage is falling apart two people, apart from car accident and apart from pregnancy (lost or gained). Sadist will never take responsibility – never. Blame and expectations and demands – this is the whole world of the sadists from the place of grandiose and sentence "I take it all," "All belongs to me." Well, no, your husband does not belong to you. If your husband does not love you and goes to his men friends – means it's not his friends who are responsible for your husband not loving you. You cannot admit that you are just not loved by him – because you would have to feel... this... – and probably as past / initial childhood pain...

Sadists hate themselves that is why they hate other people and the most who sadists hate are innocent people, because innocent people feel and are vulnerable. This is evoking in sadists again and again the inner circle of sadistic energy to be released on the innocent one. The agenda will be found and the motif will be found – no, there was no harassment in Australia. There was agenda, and an illusion as not processed pain of those who addressed the issue on the innocent scapegoat. More, there was no harassment in Australia, as there was a hidden agenda in it. The information evolved into such a scandal that this scandal reached caricature of abuse itself.

I will be very direct in here – as if somebody is peeing – who is peeing? Now – it's nature that we do not shame anyone in this example. Now what is happening if someone is peeing on the innocent? Now the innocent is wet. Whose pee is on the innocent? Who is responsible for peeing on the other? Nature of the sadist is to sadistically abuse the innocent one. Responsibility though is set on the innocent one the way I "had to pay for what was done to me behind my back" not the other way around. Sadists did not pay what they did (for at least quite a long time after the abuse was inflicted, some never pay…).

I was not accused of harassment in Australia, I was warned about that such things are happening in Australia. They could not accuse me of harassment because there was no harassment. Who was wet? Who lost face and who lost a career? Whose life was destroyed? And now – who was peeing? Sadists never take responsibility as well as sadistic communities, institutions, organisations, systems, cultures or even nations (all mentioned, they NEVER protect innocence, they only USE innocence). They 'pee' on innocent scapegoat... but it's their release, and it's victim responsibility to "pay" for this. Innocent people are dying every single day on this planet – they are dying not only by disease, not only by lack of water, not only by car accidents, not only by natures cataclysms, not only by any kind of illness, etc. Drastic numbers of people are dying because of sadists and its consequences – (no, there was no harassment in Australia). The scapegoat is never seen as a human, but rather the objectified problem and is constantly under false accusations and false assumptions for any possible, even imagined wrongdoing (there was no harassment in Australia). False accusations are hitting the level of impossible for an innocent and an innocent is accused of actions which even is not capable of doing. If someone is accusing me – who is accusing me? If I am somebody's problem, who has a problem? If I am accused of destroying somebody's marriage – whose marriage is falling apart and between whom and who does not wish to admit that was never ever loved and more, never loved their partner as well?

So let's see the next example – a rape reported at the higher organs – the person who is reporting it as a victim of it, will get punishment as false accusations – "You wanted this," "It's your fault, you went there," "Why did you go there? Now get what you asked for," "You chose this person" and more comments which are denying the reality of the criminal action which happen truly and drastic lifetime consequences for the innocent one. Let's turn this around.

Sadistic, for example, woman will accuse a man in love of harassment. She will accuse him and will be justified – "Oh, you poor woman" – it's so easy nowadays to accuse a man of harassment. And please remember – yes – and men and women can sexually harass – but many abuse the law! In this example, many innocent people – men – were accused of harassment. In some countries, accusations of harassment are used to destroy somebody's life and career, other accusations of harassment are made to revenge and from a jealousy perspective. The one in love can show affection after the seduction was there – from the "poor" woman – and now the "poor" woman with a hidden agenda is accusing him of harassment. It's sadism. And probably longer talk here is needed, while it's not the place in here to talk more about this. Accusations of harassment happen from a place of perpetrator's shame (false accuser in this case) inside that they feel rejection and lash back towards their innocent victim (falsely accused in this case) after a hidden agenda based on seduction (from false accuser). Many women use seduction towards vulnerable men to destroy their lives later on. I am here not on any side – men or women – as for me myself I was in a place of being an object in my life of people in men and women body. And no, there was no harassment in Australia. There was a group of perpetrators – and one innocent person who wished to heal early attachment wounds (*I Will Tell, Anyway!* by Ewa Lawresh). I came back from Australia fully traumatised and totally left alone in this. I started saving myself and my life, not to die literally. This is what sadistic strategic abuse looks like. Sadists project their ugliness (as inner darkness) onto the other. And will do everything to prove this ugliness from the place of hatred and rage. Sadistic strategic abuse, in fact, is based on one – to damage the innocent one privately and publicly. So it requires a lot of courage from sadistic society, and if... exists non-sadistic society and sadistic social justice and non-sadistic social justice – to stop it and help the innocent people. These innocent people are already entrapped unconsciously because if there is no help, the situation can lead to the death of the victim and anyone who will not react/respond/choose they also take responsibility for being the sadistic observers so also the sadistic passive (if there is no laughter at) participant (active sadistic participant is already the one who takes part even for the laughter at). Most people as observers think that it's not their business probably until there is a profit as a form of usage-agenda. Observers take part in this show as well as the main person who suffers (the one who suffers always lacks exact information about what is happening as it belongs to the domain of being under sadistic trauma – out of orientation). And observers are responsible for the harm and abuse which is happening to the victim (many observers meantime will steal from the person lying on the floor) taking advantage that they can...? The observer who does not act towards protection and supporting the victim under suffering – is the same sadistic perpetrator, consciously or unconsciously.

In most, if not in all of the perpetrators, there is enjoyment – inside – and do not have to be seen – it's almost like they are drawn into it... It's harmful towards innocent ones. Unfortunately, because of institutional sadistic power, the victim cannot rise over the institutions many times based on being a "problem." If there is no problem, the sadist and institutions will invent it based on themselves. Sadists also cannot believe that the victim can go away from them, and then when the sadists feel rejected, the sadists start planning their strategies to take revenge as it's based on invented by the sadists "non loyalty" from the victim. Sadists always weaken the victim mostly through psychological abuse, and they have to do this by strategies. They will not come and speak with the victim directly – of course – that they plan strategic abuse on them.

So that comes from colossal smallness and sadist's insecurities. Sadist will protect themselves by trying to protect their point of view, rigid beliefs (rather wild), and their position on the way that their actions are justified, that they had to behave a certain way as, for example, the victim was reactivated in open trauma – that the abuse as the reaction is justified on the site of the sadists – but nothing is justified on the site of the victim. And this justification as a defence will come from the perpetrator's place. Sadists will turn around (and upside down) the actions the sadists did towards the victim, accusing the victim that this is the victim who wanted to do this what is always a persecutory projection. For example, sadists will falsely accuse an innocent person of harassment while harassing the person themselves through psychological tortures in prolongation. Sadists will then accuse an innocent person of psychological abuse. At the same time, these are the sadists who were doing this. The worst is when friends of the victim will join the party for their own profit – mainly to rise on the scandal around the victim.

Chapter 9

Healing Through E.W.A.

WILD LADY – ENQUIRY, WONDER, ALLOWING (E.W.A.)
WILDNESS rather RIGIDITY (aka resilient as aligned with circulated nature)
LADY in her feminine out of rigidity whose locus of control of her own behaviour is in separation towards the outside rigid collective sadistic mind – enquiry, wonder, allowing

*I*n there is freedom as freedom is out of rigidity, freedom is in wildness.

The curiosity can ease suffering even if resistance comes while setting enquiry and asking questions (for this sadists hate questions, and they destroy innocent people's lives only for asking questions) about everything, even to the extent of wonder can ease the suffering and start the healing process. Unfortunately, sadists will never admit that they were wrong. It all was based on bla-bla-bla released noisy madness "expertized-certifications" and "diagnosis-titles" while indeed was sadistically projected from the sadistic eye of the sadistic beholder. Please consider below invented by me ways of E.W.A. as a line of being in the process of ENQUIRY, WONDER, ALLOWING:

CHILD ABUSE *[who is making a statement, about whom is the statement, to whom is the statement]*

ENQUIRY:
Why would children be interested in your husband? What if your husband is not interested in children, but you are interested in inflicting pain towards innocent children, and through this, you are accusing children of your marriage being destroyed? What if it is you who feel sexual attraction towards the innocent, and you already have had an attempt to commit crimes against children?

WONDER:
Have you ever wondered what would happen if you see that children are not interested in your husband and it is you who likes pain and who destroyed your own marriage? Have you ever wondered what would happen if you admitted you feel sexual attraction toward children and call the police and report yourself to the eye of justice? Have you ever wondered what would happen if you fully admitted you are not sure about your sexual attitude towards innocent children and your sexual thoughts while treating kids as usage for your own charge and feeling sexual arousal yourself when being around an innocent child rather than even for a moment accusing innocent one of the things you are capable of?

ALLOWING:

Would it be possible for you to accept and live with this that your husband has never loved you and you never loved him rather accusing an innocent child of destroying your marriage? Would you allow to accept and live with this that you are interested in inflicting pain on the innocent child? What would happen if you allow to feel that it is you who was touching kids sexually and inviting them to the 'innocent play games', and now you would call the police and give yourself to justice? What would happen if you allow the feeling that your husband left you emotionally because he didn't love you because of your love to inflict pain on him in his vulnerable time? Would you allow yourself to feel that it is you who is interested in inflicting pain on innocent people and destroying their lives? COULD YOU ALLOW TO FEEL THIS?

FALSE ACCUSATIONS ABUSE [who is making a statement, about whom is the statement, to whom is the statement]

ENQUIRY:

Why would an innocent person wish to harm you? What if your false accusation of harassment is your inner sexual repression to admit your own sexual desires towards the innocent one you wish to accuse? What if you are feeling harassed by your inner harasser, and this has nothing to do with the innocent one? What if you are interested in harassing the innocent one by accusing this person of harassment?

WONDER:

Have you ever wondered what would happen if you are accused of harassment yourself (and not an innocent person) from sexual repression you feel in you and only in you, and you go to jail for your own sexual harasser inside of you? Have you ever wondered what would happen if you admitted that ALL THE BLAME you direct towards an innocent one NOW you DIRECT towards yourself? Have you ever wondered what would happen if you rather putting an innocent person in jail – you would be locked forever with your inner harasser for so long that you feel that it's yours and only yours inside of you? Have you ever wondered what would happen if it is you who is interested in harassing the loved one from the place of the sadistic blame game – first by seduced invitation, then by harass persecution of the innocence?

ALLOWING:

Would it be possible for you to accept and live with this that you could let yourself feel love from an innocent one who wishes not to harm you? Would it be possible for you to accept and live with this you have inner harasser and inner sexual repressor and allow yourself to feel this fully without false accusations of the one who is walking nearby? What would happen if you allow yourself to feel that it's you who is the one who wishes to harass the loved one because you have no capacity to feel love and it's your seduced invitation to the innocent one, and when the innocent one comes closer you will backlash with your inner harasser from the place of *your sexual repressor who does not let you open place for capacity of love? COULD YOU ALLOW TO FEEL THIS?*

FALSE ACCUSATIONS ABUSE about copyrights crime [who is making a statement, about whom is the statement, to whom is the statement]

ENQUIRY:

Why someone who is a born genius would like to use your copyrighted content (about themselves) as theirs (while it's about themselves)? What if your false accusations about copyrights come from a place where it is you who is using other people's content, and you feel your hidden inner criminal who is scared to be cached? What if it's you who is committing copyright crimes, not the innocent one?

WONDER:

Have you ever wondered what could happen if it is you who were accused of using other people's content and taking it by yours, and that is why you are accusing the innocent one of this what you are doing in a hidden way? Have you ever wondered what could happen if you admitted publicly that you built all your career on the exact one you are falsely accusing of stealing the (educational) content, and you are doing it not to give full credit of your career to the one on/from whom you build this all?

ALLOWING:

Would it be possible to accept and live with this that it is you who is using other people's copyrighted content and making crimes on this rather than accusing an innocent one who is born gifted to create content on an ongoing basis and you are simply jealous and greedy? Would you allow to accept and live with this that it is you who is making content crimes (as you are an 'idiot') rather than the innocent one and that all that you earned till now on the falsely accused (exactly for the reason that the innocent one content is stolen) innocent one's content as their own life experience and according to this would you allow to admit it and send back all the earnings which belong to the innocent one who is the only owner of this content and not you? Would you allow yourself to feel that innocent people have nothing to do with your attachment to copyright stealing inside of you, and it's you who is projecting this onto others? COULD YOU ALLOW TO FEEL THIS?

FALSE ACCUSATIONS ABUSE about someone's gender [who is making a statement, about whom is the statement, to whom is the statement]

ENQUIRY:

Why would she hide who she is if she is a John? Why would she hide who she is if she is not John? Why does she not want to admit she is John? Why does she not want to admit she is not John? What if she has never identified as John, and what if it is you who identify as John? What if it is you who is hidden John? What if you are interested in becoming John? What if you are about making a coming out and admitting that you are John?

WONDER:

Have you ever wondered what could happen if you admit that it's your discreditation of a woman in a woman from your inner patriarchate? Have you ever wondered what could happen if you fully admit that you are yourself swinging between misandry and misogyny and there is no John at all? Have you ever wondered what would be the worst for you to admit you are hidden John, and not the other? Have you ever wondered what would be the scariest for you if you came out publicly as John?

ALLOWING:

Would it be possible to accept and live with this that you are hidden John rather than seeing John in the other? Would you allow to feel that you feel your inner John and your inner sexual repression and allow to feel this fully without any even moment to accuse falsely the other to be John? Would you allow yourself to feel that you are fully admitting that you are John and stop hiding? COULD YOU ALLOW TO FEEL THIS?

FALSE ACCUSATIONS ABUSE about being a cheater [who is making a statement, about whom is the statement, to whom is the statement]

ENQUIRY:

Why would she hide who she loves if she loves? Why would she hide who she does not love if she does not love? What if it is you who is cheating and lying on any possible level, from relationship level to business/corruption level, and why you never admit that you are a hidden cheater rather than pointing one finger towards the other and rest fingers towards yourself? What if she has never cheated as she has never been in a committed relationship but rather you were in a committed relationship, and you are the one who is cheating and lying to the loved one in a hidden way, saying half-truths and casual lies, and it is you who does not see a problem to cheat the one you love or even all the world? What if you are interested in casual lies, and you lie to the one with whom you are in a relationship, saying half-truths about who you feel attraction to? What if you are a cheater and a liar and not the person in their inner transformation?

WONDER:

Have you ever wondered what could happen if you admitted that it's you who cheated on your partner in your life, and you have a tendency to feel attraction to others, not only the one you love? Have you ever wondered what could happen for you to admit you are a cheater? Have you ever wondered what would be the scariest for you if you came out publicly as if you were cheating on your husband, as you have never loved your husband, but rather the one from before the marriage, and you still feel attraction towards this person whenever you meet?

ALLOWING:

Would it be possible to accept and live with this that you are a hidden cheater and liar even with casual lies within the work area rather than pointing onto the other? Would you allow to feel that you feel your inner cheater inside of you, and you stay in there, and you process your inner cheater, and you check all the lies you committed towards others who trusted you? Would you allow yourself to feel that you are not a trustworthy person yourself and admit that you are the person who should be cheated and lied to as long as you learn that it's painful for the other party if this party is innocent and trusts you? COULD YOU ALLOW TO FEEL THIS?

FALSE ACCUSATIONS ABUSE about someone's motherhood [who is making a statement, about whom is the statement, to whom is the statement]

ENQUIRY:

Why would an innocent person travel all over the world, leaving her kids and losing everything to become who she is becoming? What if your false accusations about innocent woman motherhood are all your inner accusations about your own motherhood? What if your false accusations and your blame game about an innocent mother who has nothing to do *with your motherhood and your own mother – is all about you and your own motherhood and your own mother? What if all your false accusations are based on your inner hatred of being a mother and your hatred to your own mother? What if an innocent person who wishes to have kids and loves kids the most on this planet has nothing to do with this that you do not have kids, or you cannot have kids, or you hate kids, or you abuse kids yourself, and it is you who wish never to be a mother? What if your false accusations about your mother's selfishness are all about who you deeply are?*

WONDER:

Have you ever wondered what could happen if you admit that it's your inner policing and your own blame (for your past, for your own motherhood / your own mother) that you wish to mirror towards an innocent woman in her early motherhood? Have you ever wondered what could happen if you admit you are ashamed of your own motherhood and you are the one who is 'selfish', not the innocent mom? Have you ever wondered what could happen if you free an innocent scapegoat for wrongdoing and you take full accountability to fully blame yourself and only yourself – for any wrongdoing on innocent kids? Have you ever wondered what could happen if you admit that you are the 'selfish and bad' mom yourself the way you are judging the other mom, and it is you who has never wanted to be a mom, and it is you who hates your own kids? Have you ever wondered what could happen if you admit that you are jealous and embrace your own jealousy towards an innocent mom rather than trying to destroy her public face, including destroying her life and her kids' lives?

ALLOWING:

Would it be possible to accept and live with this that someone knows better than you which motherhood way is better for her as a mother herself, and if for you staying at home mom was the best (small) place, this definitely does not have to be the best (small) place for the other mom only because she is a mom and let say for her being a mom is best to lead 'big life' as for her a place for a woman is not the place for a woman you see? Would you allow yourself to fully admit that you were not happy in your childhood with your own mother and everything that you feel towards the other innocent mother – you feel all this towards your own mother and direct this towards your own mother and leave for the sake god alone the one who is innocent? Would you allow yourself to feel your 'selfishness' of who you are fully, and it is only about you and not about the innocent one? Would you allow to admit that you falsely accused an innocent mom who was doing everything to be healthy for herself and her own kids, and it is you who have never fought for your motherhood (and you have never done anything for your own motherhood) for your own kids and you are shamefully small inside for who you are as a mother? COULD YOU ALLOW TO FEEL THIS?

FALSE ACCUSATIONS ABUSE about 'sick monster' [who is making a statement, about whom is the statement, to whom is the statement]

ENQUIRY:

Why is she hiding who she is if she is a 'sick monster'? Why is she hiding who she is if she is not a 'sick monster'? Why would she hide who she is if she is not a 'sick monster'? Why does she not want to admit she is a 'sick monster'? Why does she not want to admit she is not a 'sick monster'? What if she has never identified as a 'sick monster', and what if it is you who identifies as a 'sick monster'? What if it is you who is a hidden 'sick monster'? What if you are interested in becoming a 'sick monster'? What if you are about making a coming out and admitting publicly that you are a 'sick monster'? What if you watched too many thrillers and science fiction movies about 'sick monsters'?

WONDER:

Have you ever wondered what could happen if you admit that you are scared to become a 'sick monster' yourself as you are stepping into madness yourself? Have you ever wondered what could happen if you fully admit that you are yourself a 'sick monster' whenever you see a 'sick monster' in an innocent person? Have you ever wondered what for you would be the worst to admit to yourself that you are a 'sick monster' not the other? Have you ever wondered what would be the scariest for you if you came out publicly as a 'sick monster'?

ALLOWING:

Would it be possible to accept and live with this that you are a hidden 'sick monster' rather than see the 'sick monster' in the innocent one? Would you allow to feel that you feel *your inner 'sick monster' who is abusing innocent kids, including their sexuality and allow to feel this fully without any even moment to accuse falsely the other of being a 'sick monster' who is abusing innocent kids including their sexuality? Would you allow yourself to feel that you are fully admitting that you are a 'sick monster' and finally stop hiding? COULD YOU ALLOW TO FEEL THIS?*

REMEMBER: Sadist needs the victim (an innocent scapegoat) on the floor as they need an external problem (if sadists do not create the problem – they would realise they are a problem – it's the biggest paradox in this). Sadist needs the victim to be in toxic shame with a red face humiliated. A sadist needs an innocent person as when this innocent person is toxically shamed and belittled, so from this position of power over the sadist creates madness around the victim – it creates a circus carousel. While we need to see this with open eyes: this then creates madness over madness – mass hysteria over one innocent suffering person who is now turned into a problem – while frankly, if we turn sides, we can see that all the rest is representing patients from the psychiatric hospital rather "normal" society while the victim is the only healthy one trapped naturally in this psychiatric hospital – a healthy innocent person is now overpowered by psychiatrically diseased sadists empowered in power over.

So sadist denies sexual liveliness, which could be pure life, childlike energy in an adult or young person, the sadist is turning it into perversion with toxicity and poison inside.

It's sadists' misandry and misogyny (in both cases from sadists and from their paranoid fear – sadists will change behind the scapegoat's back – their gender – just to make the innocent one an 'idiot' and make from it a sadistic fun), prejudice and contempt towards diversity and anything that is different. Cutting off all the connections with sadistic communities is the only way to set yourself free. Sadists never change... until their lives are exchanged fully onto the same position in which they suit the innocent one – that the sadists will live the life of the innocent one who had to suffer from the sadists all or most of their life including all sadistic strategies. Cutting off sadists from life is a true stepping into your own ownership of yourself and your own life. Sadists will change under one circumstance – if they suffer everything that they did towards innocence (in this book, you had an opportunity to read many of their strategies) and as long as they inflicted sadism towards innocence (it can take a lifetime, unfortunately, as sadism is an intrinsic inner parasite which is regrowing if left out of suffering). Sadists have intrinsic maliciousness and full inner pride for being mean. This false pride is rising among those who collect themselves around sadists and laugh at the others.

The more you hate me – the more I love myself. Suffering is the only cure for sadism... if there is any other... is suffering.

Sadistic quality time is sizzling noise and stinging, hissing with mixed mockery and teasing, including gossip (which is a sadistic illusion) about people who are not there or maybe are even not alive – this way, sadists can feel better about themselves in the sadistic community bonding. This quality needs to be left by the innocent one...

Remember – the more sadists hate you – the deeper opportunity it gives you to love yourself. Take it and rise inside!

So to heal these wounds, it's very important after when all is cut off and there is a space to grow to accept for the person who is healing their own pureness as being a human and from transformation on, which is a place to meet past and feel the feelings and next is stepping into individuation. It's important to cut off all the sadistic communities from self-life – to gain own sovereignty – and to stop being controlled, stalked or even dragged out with inner life publicly for sadistic slander – which again is a crime.

Sadists will take everything, even your titles and certifications, from their own smallness so that they will do this from their own low importance and toxic inner shame and counterattack.

Sadists Have No Capacity For Love

All my sadistic perpetrators have closed hearts, and they are in full hatred towards themselves, not me! Yes, sadists hate themselves, and they hate life. No one who loves themselves is capable of anything that happened to me publicly and personally all my life through inflicted sadism from many. Sadists in hatred hate themselves, and they all live in their own sadistic stories all the time. Sadistic strategic abuse is about jealousy and hatred to protect the face of the sadistic community that they are not sluts themselves and they are hiding behind a false community face. A sadistic person can behave this way to the extent, for example, that will come to the vulnerable, innocent person who is sitting on the chair almost dying on 4th stage cancer, looking like an innocent child, fully weakened, fully dependent, fully vulnerable, looking for any resource to feel supported, to feel seen in what is happening in him and with him and looking for compassion and love. And when I am coming into this room, I see him, and his face is starting to shine from his smile. The smile is so different now, but I see him from before he was ill, when he was strong and healthy. And I see his face, shiny and happy when he sees me and welcomes me. His smile welcomes me like bright love in the aura. And the sadistic perpetrator nearby from the jealousy place looks at me from that jealousy, envy and hatred place, is looking at us – at me and at him – and with the clenched jaw with sarcasm and hatred hisses through teeth "When will be the time that you smile to me like you're smiling to her?" And the tone is so sadistic that he, from a huge, beautiful smile of the person who is very thin now hoping every single day to be again, still alive, goes into scarcity, smallness like a little boy in shock. All his face is again white like a paper.

This is not love what you have seen now through the sadistic voice. This is definitely not love beating somebody already on the floor, which happened to me while I was healing. I needed love, and I received only sadism.

Collective Mass Hysteria... Madness

Madness in sadists is never admitted, while the collective subconscious opens the entire spectrum for both in one scapegoat. From now on, we have sadists in madness as patients in a psychiatric hospital (chaos out of order is happening in the place of chaotic madness of the sadists who try to play the NORMAL one) and the innocent scapegoat who is trying to show the reality in now for them (their objectified object which is alone in the middle of it). Only what will happen – will happen only chaos out of order. While in fact, the "object" has to remove themselves. What will happen then? It depends from the past, which does not exist... yet. Don't ask sadists. They do not know either. The most important for the innocent one is to remove themselves from their madness through the simple act of signing off by cutting off.

Remember, sadists go to the end. They will destroy even if the victim is not fighting anymore, is totally unarmed, alone and passive as the wounds are too huge and too deep even to be focused on anything else any more than healing. They will destroy further as also on the example of the innocent man in the 4th stage of cancer, they will feel the trigger within themselves from their smallness, they will never admit that it is their own trigger. They will connect it with the victim (targeted object), but not themselves. They will never admit that something is happening in them, but they will point on the other person – the weak, unarmed victim (as first they will disarm the innocent to make the innocent the victim, and after this, sadists beat even more).

It looks almost like a mass hysteria that people join the statistic madness party from their own repressed denied sexuality. They go in hatred and destruction to destroy the innocent person and from this denial in themselves of their own sexuality and aliveness. They project their own sexual madness from sexual repression onto the innocent victim who is being in love like an innocent child who is natural in feeling expression, and the sadists from their sexual repression form symbolic or literal group rape by covering it through false accusations of harassment. They feel triggered by the aliveness and the love of the innocent person or a child. Sadists literally lock alive people and feeling people and definitely create from alive and feeling people the problem on this planet.

My life was destroyed. It's a fact. My life was destroyed by many individuals, groups and by many communities. It was a collective crime involving the collective subconscious, and its energy was also released. As previously mentioned, this energy is released within sadistic communities and resides there as long as sadistic communities thrive. More, as previously mentioned – sadists need release on innocence constantly, once experienced, a release is not enough as it's ongoing charge and discharge on the innocent. Most passive and non-passive watchers watched in amusement with the false joy of empowerment over the one who did not even know what was happening all this time – they all took part in collective sadistic abuse.

This what you read in this book till now it's shown

collective sadism – conscious and unconscious collective sadism towards one. It happens collectively towards the straight, cisgender woman, mom of two, fully traumatised under psychological tortures all the time who was healing wounds of sadistic sexual abuse experienced in her childhood based on brain and NS development on the program aged 0-7. What appeared publicly throughout all these years – was shown public and private sadism and drastic sadistic subconscious shadow of communities, institutions, organisations, and educational/academic level abuse in this world.

In the healing process, it's essential to let go of control and having any influence on anything, rather on self and own management on an energy level as an internal control of yourself not dependent on the outside. This is the place of the wildness that appears inside of the healthy human. My healing was based on an invented program by me mentioned before called (pathtoepichello.com). It comes from what I realised that what happened to me a few years ago was collective sadistic abuse on one person and collective sadistic abusers collected in one while trying to destroy me, they build their lives and careers on me ('collective healing' through making one scapegoat and them as the poor one – it's not healing - it's a collective abuse). They called it collective healing in few places. Power over used towards the innocence – is never collective healing – it's a collective rape. In a survival world, also Western world reputation is an outside image, outside certain face based on public position and money through how many connections you have (even the one with many connections can be an 'idiot' projecting on innocent one that is an 'idiot' – but connections are what matters the most in reputation word/construct).

In 2015 I bought a ticket to Australia with the intention to heal my own childhood and early attachment/developmental wounds (*I Will Tell, Anyway!* by Ewa Lawresh) – while the highest possible aim for me was the happiness of my 2 kids and mine – to heal and connect. My divine intentions were judged and justified by all sadists and sadistic communities/organisations/societies, even nations. I was falsely accused of travelling the world for party reasons with the etiquette of "sick monster" illusions by those whose eyes are full of thrillers and 'sick monsters'. Sadists went into such global paranoia that it reached the level of global caricature and caricature of abuse! They were in it and still did not see it.

The way they all saw it's a beautiful example of lenses of sadistic eyes of sadistic beholders... what they saw in me – they saw in themselves – not in me, so it was again "About 'me', without me" while in fact, all were without me – but all was about the sadists.

Sadists do not see anything as development as they operate on a judgemental past mode and agenda, which has nothing to do with the now and non-existing future from the place of now. A traumatised innocent person is for the sadists and sadistic communities a problem now – and as not to show the problem in communities which created the problem and are a source of the problem as communities are a symbol of motherhood itself like a 'surrounding mom' – at least should be. But observe everything that shows any sadistic community – this is who they are. All the attention is towards the possessed object – a problem they all created and named it. Can you see this?

Sadistic hypocrisy and slippery are everywhere, and this way, my all life was destroyed. Sadists are looking for a squeezed energy subconsciously in themselves to pour this out on the victim. Mostly, the way is based on external attraction and external things the victim possesses. One of the sadists came to me once and said, "Ewa, write your own books," and also added to this "Ewa, if you write a book, write about me only good things." In comparison, the same person showed about me only bad things and only behind my back. Sadists exist on thoughts. They destroyed my life based on their sadistic thoughts. Sadists, based on their sadistic thoughts, created actions based on these thoughts based on triggers by the targeted object – while, in fact, the targeted object can be only a woman walking on the street and btw triggers are inside of the body beholder and exact body beholder is responsible to take care of them. So this is a sadistic ripple effect inside of them. We need a global transformation about this to educate and raise consciousness which will transform societies and communities inside of them towards a healthy one. We need to change all the educational system while teaching children from the beginning that the thought is only the thought. We need human evolution (pathtoepichello.com, *I Will Tell, Anyway!* by Ewa Lawresh).

Chapter 0

'Postpartum Mind' FREEDOM / Wild

1. Sadists hate themselves, that's why never ever expect from sadists love, compassion and loving kindness – evolve it by yourself for yourself first. Sadists have intrinsic deep destructiveness, which is never owned by the sadists, so their blame is their blame towards themselves. Sadists don't see anyone else except themselves – all that they say is about themselves. Sadists see in anyone else sadists as sadists do not see anyone else except themselves – they see only sadism. Sadists don't see in a general human an innocent one as the sadistic eyes of the beholder are not capable of seeing anything more than sadism. Innocence sees innocence and innocence has positive psychological projections about the other – sadist has negative projections and sees in the other only negativity, and for this is falsely accusing the innocent one what they see in themselves – so after healing – don't even bother what they are saying – it's not your problem, and it was never about you. Sadists see sadism. That is why sadists accuse. If suppose sadist will tell you that they hate you, in that case, it's a separated object telling you a separated sentence

towards themselves. At the same time, they have an impression they speak to you, and as they are attached with sadism, their sentences are attached with them for them – so it's not personal as it cannot be (while for this state, you need to heal your inner pain that it's not attaching your innocence). Remember – a sadistic sentence is in the sadist's brain, which is not your brain as an innocent person's brain, let their poisoned, intoxicated brain leave with them. From this place – find a place for compassion towards sadists – it's possible after the phase – letting go (pathtoepichello.com).

2. You have to lose everything to find you and to love yourself the most, to love you – this is what came to me. It's almost cutting step by step everything, like let's say as an example is done under cancer to separate yourself from the disease on any possible level not to be affected (self-isolation is a healthy step). Step by step, until there is a safe place to heal the wounds and rise, then self-isolation is transmuted into the next phase – a safe environment.

3. To reclaim self in the face of sadism is to reclaim what the sadists are scared of the most: reclaiming divine sexuality.

4. The scapegoat of the family is always a kind of mirror for the sadists, is always the healthiest among all of them and no – nothing is wrong with you – never ever with you.

5. Remove yourself forever from sadistic family members, sadistic communities, sadistic organisations, sadistic groups and sadistic society. If needed, remove yourself from the sadistic culture-based country where is still an established sadistic system or blame game scapegoat ping-pong game through navigating targeted object based on sexually aroused topics from repressed culture.

6. Between two choices to become a certified human being or a certified teacher (put any professional title) – I choose the first one, as the second one is never connected with the first one in sadistic communities with repressed sexuality and humanity).

Sadists are in the past, they do not exist in reality and in now, so they only see who they are, and they judge sadistically from the eyes of the sadistic beholder. It's theirs, and leave it to them with them.

Anything that sadists say about an innocent person is never about the innocent person – it is always about the sadists.

Sadists hatred innocent person for a reason, as the sadists the most on this planet hatred themselves.

Sadists melt in sadism, for there is no place for love.

Sadists, none of your judgment about me can touch me as it's not about me.

Sadist, whenever you speak about me, you speak to the air poisoned by your sentences about me that is not about me but rather about you.

I truly and deeply stand for a global ecosystem without poisons in the air.

Sadist, my experience of experiencing me is not your business.

How to do this? The second part is to be continued...

This book is written this way that until you feel in your veins and to the core what is the impact of sadism on innocent, you will never ever leave the relational ground with the sadists as to leave everything you have to be fully aware to separate one from the other one. Once you set boundaries to the sadists, they will try on various levels to destroy you and your public face and take in a backstabbing way advantage on you because you are trying to be not any more their possession and their extension. Your separation as a cut-off is needed, as sadists never stop. Even if it comes to tragedy, it will still be put as it is a fault of the innocent one – no, there was no harassment in Australia. No, no one took your husband from you. No, you do not know better than me if I love my children. No, as long we do not have a work agreement, you cannot say you were working for me while being my friend at that time and now refusing to pay the money back inventing imaginary work. No, you do not have my consent that I am your pet, puppet and your extension. No, I am not a rapist, are you? No, I have never been addicted to drugs. No, I am not interested in sexual intercourse with kids, are you? No, you do not know what is better for me as you have never seen me, so how you can know what is better for me – more you have only seen you in this... No, I do not take responsibility for your misery. No, I am not ugly, are you? No, I am not your dysfunctional father. No, I am not your mother who you hate the most. No, you cannot touch me whenever you want. No, my past was not like your past, as you were never in my past, and if you claim you were in my past, you were in your own past experience, and I was in my own past experience, so we both were in two different pasts – no we were not in there together. No, you have no idea what were my intentions in life, you have no idea what are my intentions in my life, and you will never have an idea what will be my intentions in my life. No, if you are not in NOW, we cannot meet as you are not capable of seeing me. No, you cannot come to me just like that and speak to me after dehumanising me, tormenting me, humiliating me, belittling me, ridiculing me, stealing from me, achieving on me for any success while I am under torture, backstabbing me and laughing at me in your deep sadism.

This book is the first part to show you more closely what sadism is, and sadistic strategic abuse including strategies, and which way it is done from small to the global arena on HER. In the second part, you will find how to heal yourself from strategic sadistic abuse where you will find more knowledge to help yourself and become wild and free. We need human evolution (pathtoepichello.com).

After reading this book, I invite you to consider protecting yourself if you are an innocent person and protecting other innocent people, including kids (also your own), that what was done to me will never be done to the innocence.

It's a playground for the rigid fixated mind (rather wild) of the sadists. At the same time, if you were raised in a family/community where sadism was a norm, your mind and belief system and more – your eyes as eyes of the beholder will be affected by what you see and what you perceive.

Anything that is in a sadist's mind is not my problem. Anything that sadists say – is NOT about me. Understanding yourself is the key only through compassion and loving kindness. In the last years, when I was healing, I asked for loving-kindness many times – I did not receive it, though I keep asking for loving-kindness – you deserve it – if you are not the sadists. Only understanding yourself will bring freedom. First, you have to understand yourself, even if sadists never understand you. Sadistic collective strategic abuse on one was a tremendously drastic experience of slow-motion cutting my skin off – it was painful all the time. Justice is needed now as a collective cannot better through living this way what was done to me and my life and my kids' lives. All tragedy happens on a professional level, and it requires proper justice.

The less sadism, the more compassion. The less sadism, the more kindness. The less sadism, the more humanity. The less sadism, the more wildness.

Ewa Lawresh, Wild Lady Now.

About the Author

Awarded author by Raymond Aaron, Ewa has been at the forefront of the worldwide movement: – to have the right to exist on this planet rather than being persecuted; – divine sexuality based on divine love rather than being prosecuted *(love is always love; if it's not love – it's death);* – using your voice rather keeping silence (including mutism/people with special needs). The award-winning author currently lives in the UK with her 2 kids but travels across the world conducting public speeches on big stages to raise awareness about mental health and prevention of domestic and international violence against innocent people inflicted mainly by institutionalisation and research on innocence from sadistic societies / communities / organisations / legal / educational system. We need a global transformation which will change towards a healthy society based on loving kindness, compassion, under-standing and non-judgemental inclusion of all possible diversity on the spectrum of being a human as a healthy ecosystem based on humanity. We need to start from the most innocent and vulnerable – those who will carry living on this planet when we are not here anymore – our children, teenagers and young people teaching them from the beginning that: – the thought is only a thought (including *judgement*) which is created in the mind of the exact body beholder and that feelings are to be felt in the exact body of the exact beholder. All is about human evolution as inner transformation to reach wholeness (Path to Epic Hello – pathtoepichello.com). Human rights are for humans, and if a human is a human, that means a human is not a product. Product rights are product rights (including kidnapping).

Ewa is operating on the following online portfolios:

www.wildladynow.com

www.pathtoepicjello.com

www.iwilltellanyway.com

www.voiceofdivine.com

where she works around domestic and international establishments based on human evolution. Ewa is an aspiring writer, artist, inventor and entrepreneur who is coaching "one on many" internationally lives from authenticity and wholeness.

If you wish to support Ewa from the genuine place standing for her human rights and her global injustice experienced till now while Ewa was under inflicted pain through sadistic collective strategic abuse, please send your donations to her PayPal account: wildladynow@gmail.com

Titles of books by Ewa Lawresh

Lawresh, E., *I Will Tell, Anyway! Games of the First Sadist.* Oxford, 2021. ISBN 978-1-8384133-0-9

Lawresh, E., *Wild Lady. Freedom From Sadistic Strategic Abuse.* Oxford, 2022. ISBN – 978-1-8384133-9-2

Printed in Great Britain
by Amazon